LOVE, POWER, AND JUSTICE

Love, Power, and Justice

ONTOLOGICAL ANALYSES AND ETHICAL APPLICATIONS

PAUL TILLICH

OXFORD UNIVERSITY PRESS

LONDON   OXFORD   NEW YORK

OXFORD UNIVERSITY PRESS

Oxford   London   Glasgow

New York   Toronto   Melbourne   Wellington

Nairobi   Dar es Salaam   Cape Town

Kuala Lumpur   Singapore   Jakarta   Hong Kong   Tokyo

Delhi   Bombay   Calcutta   Madras   Karachi

Copyright 1954 by Oxford University Press, Inc.

Library of Congress Catalogue Card Number: 54-6522

Given as Firth Lectures in Nottingham, England

And as Sprunt Lectures in Richmond, Virginia

First published by Oxford University Press, London, 1954

First issued as an Oxford University Press paperback, 1960

printing, last digit: 29 28 27 26 25 24 23 22 21

Printed in the United States of America

TO
MY SISTER

PREFACE

THIS book contains the lectures I gave first in
Nottingham, England, when the Firth Foundation
asked me to deliver the first series of Firth Lectures,
and to take as my subject the problems of Love, Power,
and Justice. In spite of some hesitation on my part,
rooted in the almost insuperable difficulty of dealing
with such large problems in only six lectures, I finally
accepted. For I realized that one cannot work constructively in theology, philosophy, and ethics without
encountering at every step the concepts which constitute the subject of these lectures: Love, Power, and
Justice.

A second step on my way to the publication of this
book was the request of the Christian Gauss Foundation in Princeton, U.S.A., to direct a seminar on the
concepts of Love, Power, and Justice with a highly
selective group of professors, advanced students, and
other intellectual leaders. The criticism I received on
this occasion was very helpful when it came to the
third step on the way to the publication of this book.

The third step was the request of the Sprunt Foundation in the Union Theological Seminary, Richmond,
Virginia, to give seven Sprunt Lectures about the subject of my Firth Lectures. Since it was a kind of emergency situation—the originally designated lecturer was

prevented from coming—the University of Nottingham agreed that as I rewrote the lectures, correcting and enlarging their original form, I should be free to use them in accepting the invitation of the Sprunt Foundation. The difficulty connected with this task surpassed almost everything I have experienced within my academic career. The only way out was to limit my scope to a basic ontological analysis of the three concepts and to some applications of the concepts, elaborated through this procedure. The last three chapters give such applications, while the preceding three attempt an ontological analysis of each of the three concepts, showing their common root in the nature of being itself. The first chapter is a critical introduction to the problem raised by the confused state of the dissension concerning love, power, and justice.

The lectures out of which this book has grown carry the weight of two important Lecture Foundations, the Firth Foundation and the Sprunt Foundation, a weight almost too heavy for one lecturer and one series of lectures. I want to thank both Foundations for the honour of being their lecturer as well as for the welcome occasion and the wholesome compulsion to deal with all the problems of these lectures in a more direct and systematic way than I had ever done before.

P. T.

New York
April 1953.

CONTENTS

LOVE, POWER, AND JUSTICE

I
PROBLEMS, CONFUSIONS, METHOD

Intrinsic problems of love, power, and justice

ONE cannot work constructively in theology or philosophy without encountering at every step the concepts which constitute the subject of these lectures, love, power, and justice. They appear in decisive places in the doctrine of man, in psychology and sociology, they are central in ethics and jurisprudence, they determine political theory and educational method, they cannot be avoided even in mental and bodily medicine. Each of the three concepts in itself and all three in their relation to each other are universally significant. Therefore it is necessary, though almost impossible, to make them the subject of a special inquiry. It is necessary because no analysis and no synthesis in any of the spheres in which they appear can avoid referring to them in a significant and often in a decisive way. Yet it is almost impossible because nobody is an expert in all the realms in which the three concepts play an outstanding role. Therefore one must ask whether there is a root meaning in each of these concepts, determining their use in the different situations to which they are applied. Such a basic meaning would precede in logical validity the variety of meanings which could be derived from it. Therefore the search for the basic meaning of love, power, and justice individually must be our first task, and it must be carried out as a part of the search for the basic meaning of all those concepts which are universally present in man's cognitive encounter with his world. Traditionally they are called principles, structural elements, and categories of being. Their elaboration is the work of ontology. Ontology is the way in which the root meaning of all principles and also of the three concepts of our subject can be found. It is the way which I intend to take in this and the subsequent chapters. Ontologically we shall ask for the root meaning of love and of power and of justice. And if we do so, we may discover not only their particular meanings but also their structural relation to each other and to being as such. If we could achieve this task, we would be able to judge the many ways in which the intrinsic problems as well as the mutual relations of the three concepts have been defined. And we would be able to give ourselves a more basic description of their mutual relationship.

It is, however, not only the variety of meanings in which the concepts of love, power, and justice are used; it is also the confused state of the discussion of each of them and the even more confused state of the discussion of their mutual relations which puts an almost insuperable hurdle before us. Nevertheless, we must try, and we must first survey the problems and confusions which we shall encounter at every step of our inquiry.

It is unusual to take the word 'confusion' into the title of a chapter. But if one has to write about love, power, and justice the unusual becomes natural. The warning and the help of the semanticist is perhaps in no realm so much needed as in the jungle of ambiguities which has grown up through the lack of conceptual control and the abundance of emotional drive in the sphere which is circumscribed by love, power, and justice. The confusions are partly intrinsic and partly relational.

In spite of all the misuses to which the word *love* is subjected, in literature and daily life, it has not lost its emotional power. It elicits a feeling of warmth, of passion, of happiness, of fulfilment, whenever it is used. It brings to mind past or present or anticipated occasions of loving or being loved. Its root meaning, therefore, seems to be an emotional state which like all emotions cannot be defined, but which must be described in its qualities and expressions and is not a matter of intention or demand but of happening or gift. If this were so, love could be kept within the sphere of affections, and it could be discussed as one affection among others—as it was, for instance, by Spinoza. But it is significant that Spinoza, when he comes to his final statements about the nature of the divine substance and about the many ways in which man participates in it, speaks of man's intellectual love towards God as the love with which God loves himself. In other words, he elevates love out of the emotional into the ontological realm. And it is well known that from Empedocles and Plato to Augustine and Pico, to Hegel and Schelling, to Existentialism and depth psychology, love has played a central ontological role.

There is another interpretation of love which is neither emotional nor ontological but ethical. In one of the determining documents of Judaism, Christianity and all Western civilization, the word love is combined with the imperative 'thou shalt'. The Great Commandment demands of everyone the total love of God and the love of one's neighbour according to the measure of man's natural self-affirmation. If love is emotion, how can it be demanded? Emotions cannot be demanded. We cannot demand them of ourselves. If we try, something artificial is produced which shows the traits of what had to be suppressed in its production. Repentance, intentionally produced, hides self-complacency in perversion. Love, intentionally produced, shows indifference or hostility in perversion. This means: love as an emotion cannot be commanded. Either love is something other than emotion or the Great Commandment is meaningless. There must be something at the basis of love as emotion which justifies both its ethical and its ontological interpretation. And it may well be that the ethical nature of love is dependent on its ontological nature, and that the ontological nature of love gets its qualifications by its ethical character. But if all this is valid—and we shall try to show that it is valid—the question arises as to how these interpretations of love are related to the fact that love appears in the shape of the most passionate of emotions.

This question, however, cannot be answered without considering another set of problems, which is not only extremely important in itself, but which also has come into the foreground of theological and ethical interest in the last decades. It is the question of the qualities of love. In the public discussion which centres around the distinction between *erōs* and *agapē* (the earthly and the heavenly love in Renaissance symbolism), the qualities of love are called types of love, and in extreme cases one even denies that the same word 'love' should be applied to these contradictory types. But I have learned, while elaborating these lectures, that there are not types but qualifications of love, since the different qualities are present, by efficiency or deficiency, in every act of love. This insight, however, does not make the distinction of the qualities of love less important. If, as I shall suggest, one has to distinguish the *libido*, the *philia*, the *erōs*, the *agapē* qualities of love one must ask: how are they related to each other? What is meant if one speaks of love without qualification?

5

Which quality of love is adequate to the Great Commandment? Which to its emotional quality?

Whenever the word 'love' is used one also speaks of self-love. How is self-love related to the qualities of love, to its ontological and to its ethical character? First of all one must ask whether self-love is a meaningful concept at all. Considering that love presupposes a separation of the loving subject and the loved object, is there such a separation in the structure of self-consciousness? I am very doubtful about using the term 'self-love', and if it is used, about using it in any except a metaphorical sense. Besides this terminological question, one must ask how the different qualities of love are related to what is metaphorically called self-love, and how it is related to the ethical and to the ontological nature of love.

This survey of the problems and confusions, connected with the use of the term 'love' is equalled by a survey of the confusions and problems connected with the public discussion of the concept of power. I may tell an anecdote which has more symbolic than analytical meaning. I have been warned not to announce a lecture on 'Love, Power, and Justice' in the United States, because power would be understood as the product of the electrical power companies, and justice as the fight against the policy of the Federal Government to provide for cheap electrical power by the regulation of rivers according to the pattern of the Tennessee

Valley Authority. Power in the sense presupposed by this story is electrical power. In the same way the term 'power' can be applied to all physical causes, although theoretical physics has got rid of this anthropomorphic symbol and has replaced it by mathematical equations. But even present-day physics speaks of power-fields in order to describe the basic structures of the material world. This is at least an indication of the significance the term 'power' has even in the most abstract analysis of physical occurrences.

Physicists are usually conscious of the fact that they use an anthropomorphic metaphor when they use the term 'power'. Power is a sociological category and from there it is transferred to nature (just as is law, as we shall see later). But the term 'metaphor' does not solve the problem. We must ask, how is it possible that both physics and social science use the same word, 'power'? There must be a point of identity between the structure of the social and the structure of the physical world. And this identity must be manifest in the common use of the term 'power'. There is, however, only one way of discovering the root meaning of power, namely to ask about its ontological foundation. And this, of course, is one of the purposes of these lectures.

Within the social realm the meaning of power is burdened by another ambiguity, the relation of power and force. This duality is almost exclusively restricted to the human sphere. For only in man, that is in the being whose nature is finite freedom, the distinction of power and force is meaningful. One speaks of 'power politics', and one often does so with moral indignation. But this is the consequence of mere confusion. Politics and power politics are one and the same thing. There are no politics without power, neither in a democracy nor in a dictatorship. Politics and power politics point to the same reality. It does not matter which term you are using. Unfortunately, however, the term 'power politics' is used for a special type of politics, namely that in which power is separated from justice and love, and is identified with compulsion. This confusion is possible because there is indeed a compulsory element in the actuality of power. But this is only one element, and if power is reduced to it and loses the form of justice and the substance of love, it destroys itself and the politics based on it. Only penetration into the onto-logical roots of power can overcome the ambiguities in the relation of power and compulsion.

If power is distinguished from compulsion the question arises whether there is a power which is neither physical nor psychological, but spiritual. Compulsion uses both physical and psychological means in order to exercise power, most conspicuously in the terror methods of dictatorships. No compulsion at all is pre-supposed in spiritual power. Nevertheless, one assumes that spiritual power is the greatest, that it is the ulti-mate power. One does so whenever one says that God is Spirit. The question then is, how does spiritual power work, how is it related to physical and psychological power, and how is it related to the compulsory element of power?

For hundreds of years people have discussed the meaning of the third of our concepts: justice. Since earliest times justice has been symbolized in myth and poetry, in sculpture and architecture. Nevertheless, its meaning is not unambiguous. On the contrary, its legal meaning seems to be contradicted by its ethical one, and both the legal and the ethical meaning seem to be in conflict with its religious meaning. Legal justice, moral righteousness, and religious justification seem to struggle with each other. Aristotle speaks of justice as a proportion, both in distribution and retribution. This raises several problems. First, one must ask whether the terms 'distributive' and 'retributive justice' constitute a valid distinction. Distributive justice gives goods to everybody according to his just claim; and his just claim is determined by his social status, which is partly dependent on the status he has received by historical destiny in universe and society, and partly by his own merits in actualizing his status and its potentialities. Retributive justice takes place if he diminishes his status and its just claims by not fulfilling its potentialities or by acting against the social or cosmic order in which his status is rooted. Retributive justice then appears as punishment and produces the problem of the meaning of punishment and its relation to justice. Is punishment a purpose in itself, determined by retributive justice, or is it the negative implication of distributive justice and determined by it? Only an ontological consideration of justice can lead towards an answer. The same is true of the meaning of justice as proportion. The term 'proportional justice' implies degrees of justified claims. It presupposes a hierarchy of standing and claims for a just distribution. On the other hand, the word 'justice' implies an element of equality. How is the hierarchical element in proportional justice related to the equalitarian element in it? The question becomes even more difficult if we consider the fact that the status of a being in universe and society is subject to continuous changes. The dynamic character of life seems to exclude the concept of a just claim; it seems to undercut even the idea of proportional justice. Is there a type of justice which transcends and restricts the kind of justice described by Aristotle? Can perhaps the proportional element be taken into a dynamic-creative type of justice? This again demands assumptions about the relation of the static to the dynamic character of being; it demands ontological assumptions.

None of the three concepts, love, power, and justice can be defined, described and understood in their varied meanings without an ontological analysis of their root meanings. None of the confusions and ambiguities in the use of the three concepts can be removed, none of the problems intrinsic in them can be solved without an answer to the question: How are love, power, and justice rooted in the nature of being as such?

Relational problems of love, power, and justice

The ambiguities in the meaning of love, power, and justice have confusing consequences and produce new problems as soon as the relation of the three concepts to each other is considered. Love and power are often contrasted in such a way that love is identified with a resignation of power and power with a denial of love. Powerless love and loveless power are contrasted. This, of course, is unavoidable if love is understood from its emotional side and power from its compulsory side. But such an understanding is error and confusion. It was this misinterpretation which induced the phil-osopher of the 'will-to-power' (i.e. Nietzsche) to reject radically the Christian idea of love. And it is the same misinterpretation which induces Christian theologians to reject Nietzsche's philosophy of the 'will-to-power' in the name of the Christian idea of love. In both cases an ontology of love is missing and in the second case power is identified with social compulsion. In the same period the theological school which has been created by Albrecht Ritschl dominated the field of Protestant theology. The anti-metaphysical bias of this school caused it to contrast the love of God with His power in such a way that the power actually disappeared and God became identified with love in its ethical meaning. The consequence was an ethical theism which neglected almost completely the divine mystery and majesty. God as the power of being was discarded as a pagan invasion. The trinitarian symbolism was dissolved. The kingdom of God was reduced to the ideal of an ethical community. Nature was excluded because power was excluded. And power was excluded because the question of being was excluded. For if the question of being is asked and concepts like love and power are seen in the light of the ontological question, the unity of their root meanings can become visible. Yet most important are the problems in social ethics which result from the confrontation of love and power. One could say that constructive social ethics are impossible as long as power is looked at with distrust and love is reduced to its emotional or ethical quality. Such a division leads to a rejection of or indifference to the political realm on the side of religion. And it leads to the separation of the political from the religious and the ethical and to the politics of mere compulsion on the political side. Constructive social ethics presuppose that one is aware of the element of love in structures of power and of the element of power without which love becomes chaotic surrender. It is the ontological analysis of love and power which must produce this awareness.

The problems and confusions which characterize the discussion of love in its relation to power, characterize equally the discussion of love in its relation to justice. One does not usually contrast love with justice in the way in which one contrasts love with power. But it is commonly accepted that love adds something to justice that justice cannot do by itself. Justice, one says, demands that an inherited fortune is distributed in equal parts amongst those who have the same legal claim. But love may induce one of the heirs to surrender his right to one of the other heirs. In this case he acts in a way which is not demanded by justice, but which may be demanded by love. Love transcends justice. This seems rather evident, but it is not! If justice is not limited to proportional distribution, the act of resignation might have been an act of non-proportional justice, or it might have been an act of injustice against oneself, as in the first act of Shakespeare's *King Lear*, when Lear surrenders all his powers to his daughters. The relation of love to justice cannot be understood in terms of an addition to justice which does not change its character. Only an ontology of justice can describe the true relation of the root concepts. Another example supports this view. A man may say to another: 'I know your criminal deed and, according to the demand of justice, I should bring you to trial, but because of my Christian love I let you go.' Through this leniency, which is wrongly identified with love, a person may be driven towards a thoroughly criminal career. This means that he has received neither justice nor love, but injustice, covered by sentimentality. He might have been saved by having been brought to trial after his first fall. In this case the act of being just would have been the act of love. In classical theology the tension between love and justice is symbolized in the doctrine of atonement as developed by Anselm of Canterbury. According to Anselm, God Himself must find a way to escape the consequences of His retributive justice which conflicts with His merciful love. He is subject to the law of justice which is given by Himself. And this law would cause the eternal death of all men in spite of His desire to save man according to His love. The solution is the undeserved, substitutional death of the God-man, Jesus Christ. In spite of its theological weakness this remained the predominant doctrine in Western Christianity because of its psychological power. It implies the onto-logical insight, which it explicitly contradicts, that ultimately love must satisfy justice in order to be real love, and that justice must be elevated into unity with love in order to avoid the injustice of eternal destruction. But this is not manifest in the legal form in which the doctrine is developed.

Another point in which the impossibility of the

'theory of addition' of love and justice becomes visible is the relation of love and justice to the concrete situation. Justice is expressed in principles and laws none of which can ever reach the uniqueness of the concrete situation. Every decision which is based on the abstract formulation of justice alone is essentially and inescapably unjust. Justice can be reached only if both the demand of the universal law and the demand of the particular situation are accepted and made effective for the concrete situation. But it is love which creates participation in the concrete situation. It would be completely wrong to say that love must be added to justice if the uniqueness of the situation is to be reached. For this would mean that justice as such is impossible. Actually the situation shows that justice is just because of the love which is implicit in it. But this can be understood fully only in the context of an ontological analysis of the root meanings of both love and justice.

The weight of the problems and the dangerous character of the confusions is equally obvious when we finally confront power and justice. It is in this realm of problems that the relation of law and order to justice and of all of them to power is discussed and more often confused than illuminated. The first question is: Who gives the law in which justice is supposed to be expressed? To give a law is the basic manifestation of power. But if a group which has power gives laws, how are they related to justice? Are they not simply the expression of the will to power of this group? The Marxist theory of the State asserts that the laws of the State are tools which give social control to a ruling group. The origin of its power may be military invasion or it may be socio-economic stratification. In both cases justice is possible only if the State has withered away and has been replaced by an administration without political power. The justice of the ruling class is injustice and, if defended, ideology. The laws it gives preserve a social order, and as long as there is no alternative social order, the laws of the ruling classes are better than chaos. The more cynical representatives of this theory interpret justice exclusively as a function of power and in no way as its judge. They accept the Marxist analysis without the Marxist expectation, and reduce justice completely to a function of power. In reaction against this removal of justice as an ultimate principle a theory has been developed which tries to separate justice from power completely and to establish it as a self-contained system of valid judgements. Justice is an absolute, without any relation to structures of power. The positive law, derived from the principles of the natural or rational law, does not express what is, but it demands what should be. Irrespective of power it commands and expects obedience because of its intrinsic validity. It does not express but it judges power. The contrast of these two theories about the relation of power to justice reveals the difficulty of the problem and the necessity of an ontological research into the root meanings of power and justice.

As announced before, I have led you into a jungle of problems and confusions, and, at every point, I have indicated the way out; namely, the ontological analysis of love, power, and justice. The nature of this method will be discussed in the following chapter in connexion with an attempt to give an ontological interpretation of the meaning of love.

II

BEING AND LOVE

The ontological question

ALL problems of love, power, and justice drive us to
an ontological analysis. The confusions cannot be
cleared up, nor can the problems be solved without an
answer to the question: In what way is each of these
concepts rooted in being-itself? And the question of
being-itself is the ontological question. It is, therefore,
appropriate that, before dealing with the ontological
roots of each of our concepts, we ask: What does
'root' in this sense mean? What is the 'root-meaning'
of a concept? How is the ontological question to be
raised and how can it be answered?

Ontology is the elaboration of the 'logos' of the
'on', in English of the 'rational word' which grasps
'being as such'. It is hard for the modern mind to
understand the Latin *esse-ipsum*, being-itself, or the
Greek ὄν ᾗ ὄν, being-in-so-far-as-it-is-being. We all are
nominalists by birth. And as nominalists we are inclined
to dissolve our world into things. But this inclination
is an historical accident and not an essential necessity.
The concern of the so-called realists of the Middle Ages
was to maintain the validity of the universals as genuine
expressions of being. It is however not realism to which

I want you to turn from the naïve nominalism in which the modern world lives, but I want you to turn to something older than both nominalism and realism: to the philosophy which asks the question of being before the split into universal essences and particular contents. This philosophy is older than any other. It is the most powerful element in all great philosophies of the past, and it has come into its own in the important philosophical attempts of our period. It is the philosophy which asks the question: What does it mean that something *is*? What are the characteristics of everything that participates in being? And this is the question of ontology.

Ontology does not try to describe the nature of beings, either in their universal, generic qualities, or in their individual, historical manifestations. It does not ask about stars and plants, animals and men. It does not ask about events and those who act within these events. This is the task of scientific analysis and historical description. But ontology asks the simple and infinitely difficult question: What does it mean *to be*? What are the structures, common to everything that is, to everything that participates in being? One cannot avoid this question by denying that there are such common structures. One cannot deny that being is one and that the qualities and elements of being constitute a texture of connected and conflicting forces. This texture is one, in so far as it *is* and gives the power of being to each of its qualities and elements. It is one but it is neither a dead identity nor a repetitious sameness. It is one in the manifoldness of its texture. Ontology is the attempt to describe this texture, to reveal its hidden nature through the word which belongs to being and in which being comes to itself. Yet let us not make a mistake: ontology does not describe the infinite variety of beings, living and dead, subhuman and human. Ontology characterizes the texture of being itself, which is effective in everything that is, in all beings, living and dead, subhuman and human. Ontology precedes every other cognitive approach to reality. It precedes all sciences, not always historically, but always in logical dignity and basic analysis. One does not need to look back at past centuries or far-removed parts of the world to discover the primacy of the ontological question. The best method for discovering it to-day is a careful analysis of the writings of leading anti-ontological philosophers or of anti-philosophical scientists and historians. One will easily discover that on almost every page of the writings of these men a certain number of basic ontological concepts are used, but surreptitiously and therefore often wrongly. One cannot escape ontology if one wants to know! For knowing means recognizing something as being. And being is an infinitely involved texture, to be described by the never-ending task of ontology.

It is decisive for our purpose in these chapters to notice that the early philosophers, when they tried to speak in terms of the *logos* about the nature of being, could not do it without using words like love, power, and justice or synonyms for them. Our triad of terms points to a trinity of structures in being itself. Love, power, and justice are metaphysically speaking as old as being itself. They precede everything that is, and they cannot be derived from anything that is. They have ontological dignity. And before having received ontological dignity they had mythological meaning. They were gods before they became rational qualities of being. The substance of their mythological meaning is reflected in their ontological significance. *Dikē*, the goddess of justice, receives Parmenides when he is introduced into truth itself. For there is no truth without the form of truth, namely justice. And being-itself, according to the same philosopher, is kept within the bondage of eternal laws. The *logos* of being is the power which keeps the world going and the city alive, according to Heraclitus, and Mind is the divine power which swings the wheel of being, according to Xenophanes. According to Empedocles, it is hate and love, separation, and reunion which determine the movements of the elements. Love, power, and justice are ever repeated subjects of ontology. There is hardly a leading philosopher who does not put them into the very foundations of his thought. In Plato we find the doctrine of *erōs* as the power which drives to the union with the true and the good itself. In his interpretation of the ideas as the essences of everything, he sees them as the 'powers of being'. And justice for him is not a special virtue, but the uniting form of the individual and the social body. In Aristotle we find the doctrine of the universal *erōs* which drives everything towards the highest form, the pure actuality which moves the world not as a cause (*kinoumenon*) but as the object of love (*erōmenon*). And the movement he describes is a movement from the potential to the actual, from *dynamis* to *energeia*, two concepts which include the concept of power. In the line of thought which leads from Augustine to Boehme, Schelling, and Schopenhauer it is the half-symbolic use of the concept 'will' in which the element of power is preserved, while the emphasis on the *logos* of being in all of them preserves the element of justice, and the ontology of love in Augustine and all his followers shows the primacy of love in relation to power and justice. It is well known to the students of Hegel that he started in his early fragments as a philosopher of love, and it can be said without exaggeration that Hegel's dialectical scheme is an abstraction from his concrete intuition into the nature of love as separation and reunion. It should also be mentioned that in the recent psychotherapeutic literature the relation between power-drive and love is in the foreground of interest. Love has been more and more acknowledged as the answer to the question implied in anxiety and neurosis.

The historical survey shows the basic ontological significance of the triad of concepts we have to discuss. Now the question of method arises: How is ontology distinguished from what has been called metaphysics? The answer is that ontology is the foundation of metaphysics, but not metaphysics itself. Ontology asks the question of being, i.e. of something that is present to everybody at every moment. It is never 'speculative' in the (unjustified) bad sense of the word, but it is always descriptive, describing the structures which are presupposed in any encounter with reality. Ontology is descriptive, not speculative. It tries to find out which the basic structures of being are. And being is given to everybody who is and who therefore participates in being-itself. Ontology, in this sense, is analytical. It analyses the encountered reality, trying to find the structural elements which enable a being to participate in being. It separates those elements of the real which are generic or particular from those elements which are constitutive for everything that is and therefore are universal. It leaves the former to the special sciences or to metaphysical constructions, it elaborates the latter through critical analysis. Obviously this task is an infinite one, because the encounter with reality is inexhaustible and always reveals qualities of being, the ontological foundation of which must be investigated.

Secondly, one must ask: Is there a way of verifying ontological judgements? There is certainly not an experimental way, but there is an experiential way. It is the way of an intelligent recognition of the basic ontological structures within the encountered reality, including the process of encountering itself. The only answer, but a sufficient answer, which can be given to the question of ontological verification is the appeal to intelligent recognition. For the following analysis this appeal is made. Finally, the question of a method cannot be answered before the method is applied successfully or unsuccessfully. Method and content cannot be separated.

An ontology of love

All problems concerning the relation of love to power and justice, individually as well as socially, become insoluble if love is basically understood as emotion. Love would be a sentimental addition to power and justice, ultimately irrelevant, unable to change either the laws of justice or the structures of power. Most of the pitfalls in social ethics, political theory, and education are due to a misunderstanding of the ontological character of love. On the other hand, if love is understood in its ontological nature, its relation to justice and power is seen in a light which reveals the basic unity of the three concepts and the conditioned character of its conflicts.

Life is being in actuality and love is the moving power of life. In these two sentences the ontological nature of love is expressed. They say that being is not actual without the love which drives everything that is towards everything else that is. In man's experience of love the nature of life becomes manifest. Love is the drive towards the unity of the separated. Reunion presupposes separation of that which belongs essentially together. It would, however, be wrong to give to separation the same ontological ultimacy as to reunion. For separation presupposes an original unity. Unity embraces itself and separation, just as being comprises itself and non-being. It is impossible to unite that which is *essentially* separated. Without an ultimate be-longingness no union of one thing with another can be conceived. The absolutely strange cannot enter into a communion. But the estranged is striving for reunion. In the loving joy about the 'other one' the joy about one's own self-fulfilment by the other is also present. That which is absolutely strange to me cannot add to my self-fulfilment; it can only destroy me if it touches the sphere of my being. Therefore love cannot be described as the union of the strange but as the reunion of the estranged. Estrangement presupposes original oneness. Love manifests its greatest power there where it overcomes the greatest separation. And the greatest separation is the separation of self from self. Every self is self-related and a complete self is completely self-related.

It is an independent *centre*, indivisible and impenetrable, and therefore is rightly called an individual.

The separation of a completely individualized being from any other completely individualized being is itself complete. The centre of a completely individualized being cannot be entered by any other individualized being, and it cannot be made into a mere part of a higher unity. Even as a part it is indivisible and it is as such more than a part. Love reunites that which is self-centred and individual. The power of love is not something which is added to an otherwise finished process, but life has love in itself as one of its constitutive elements. It is the fulfilment and the triumph of love that it is able to reunite the most radically separated beings, namely individual persons. The individual person is both most separated and the bearer of the most powerful love.

We have rejected the attempt to restrict love to its emotional element. But there is no love without the emotional element, and it would be a poor analysis of love which did not take this element into consideration. The question is only how to relate it to the ontological definition of love. One can say that love as an emotion is the anticipation of the reunion which takes place in every love-relation. Love, like all emotions, is an expression of the total participation of the being which is in an emotional state. In the moment in which one is in love the fulfilment of the desire for reunion is anticipated and the happiness of this reunion is experienced in imagination. This means that the emotional element in love does not precede the others ontologically but that the ontologically founded movement to the other one expresses itself in emotional ways. Love is a passion: this assertion implies that there is a passive element in love, namely the state of being driven towards reunion. Infinite passion for God as described by Kierkegaard is, no less than the sexual passion, a consequence of the objective situation, namely of the state of separation of those who belong together and are driven towards each other in love.

The ontology of love is tested by the experience of love fulfilled. There is a profound ambiguity about this experience. Fulfilled love is, at the same time, extreme happiness and the end of happiness. The separation is overcome. But without the separation there is no love and no life. It is the superiority of the person-to-person relationship that it preserves the separation of the self-centred self, and nevertheless actualizes their reunion in love. The highest form of love and that form of it which distinguishes Eastern and Western cultures is the love which preserves the individual who is both the subject and the object of love. In the loving person-to-person relationship Christianity manifests its superiority to any other religious tradition.

The ontology of love leads to the basic assertion that love is one. This contradicts the main trend in the recent discussions of the nature of love. They were useful in so far as they directed the attention to the different qualities of love. But they were and are misleading in so far as they consider the differences of qualities as differences of types. The error was not that one distinguished the qualities of love—on the contrary, *more* distinctions should have been made in what was often comprehended under the name *erōs*. The error was that one did not start with an understanding of love as one. Such an understanding, of course, would have led to an ontological analysis. For only the relation of love to being as such can reveal its fundamental character.

If love in all its forms is the drive towards the reunion of the separated, the different qualities of the one nature of love become understandable. Traditionally *epithymia* ('desire') is considered the lowest quality of love. It is identified with the desire to sensual self-fulfilment. There is a strong interest on the part of philosophical and theological moralists in establishing a complete gap between this quality and those which are supposed to be higher and essentially different. On the other hand, there is a tendency on the naturalist side to reduce all the other qualities of love to the *epithymia* quality. A solution of this problem is only possible in the light of the ontological interpretation of love. First of all it must be said that *libido*—to use the Latin word—is misunderstood if it is defined as the desire for pleasure. This hedonistic definition is, like hedonism generally, based on a wrong psychology which itself is the consequence of a wrong ontology. Man strives to reunite himself with that to which he belongs and from which he is separated. And this is true not only of man but of all living beings. They desire food, movement, growth, participation in a group, sexual union, etc. The fulfilment of these desires is accompanied by pleasure. But it is not the pleasure as such which is desired, but the union with that which fulfils the desire. Certainly, fulfilled desire is pleasure, and unfulfilled desire is pain. But it is a distortion of the actual processes of life if one derives from these facts the pain-pleasure principle in the sense that life essentially consists of fleeing from pain and striving for pleasure. Whenever this happens life is corrupted. Only a perverted life follows the pain-pleasure principle. Unperverted life strives for that of which it is in want, it strives for union with that which is separated from it, though it belongs to it. This analysis should remove the prejudice towards libido, and it can give criteria for the partial acceptance, partial rejection of Freud's libido theory. In so far as Freud describes libido as the desire of the individual to get rid of his tensions, he has described the perverted form of libido. And he has acknowledged this implicitly (though not intentionally) by deriving the death-instinct from the infinite, never fulfilled libido. Freud describes man's libido in its perverted, self-estranged stage. But his description, in which he joins many Puritans (old and new ones who would be embarrassed by this alliance) misses the meaning of libido as the normal drive towards vital self-fulfilment. In the light of this analysis it is justified to say that *epithymia* is a quality which is not lacking in any love relation. To this extent the naturalists are right. But they are wrong if they interpret libido or *epithymia* as the striving for pleasure for the sake of pleasure.

The attempts to establish an absolute contrast between *agapē* and *erōs* usually presuppose an identification of *erōs* and *epithymia*. Certainly, there is *epithymia* in every *erōs*. But *erōs* transcends *epithymia*. It strives for a union with that which is a bearer of values because of the values it embodies. This refers to the beauty we find in nature, to the beautiful and the true in culture, and to the mystical union with that which is the source of the beautiful and the true. Love drives towards union with the forms of nature and culture and with the divine sources of both. This *erōs* is united with *epithymia* if *epithymia* is the desire for vital self-fulfilment and not for the pleasure resulting from this union. This valuation of *erōs* is attacked from two sides. Love as *erōs* is depreciated by those theologians who depreciate culture and by those who deny a mystical element in man's relation to God. But it is a rather self-defying attitude if somebody depreciates culture and does it in terms of culture, if he, e.g., uses millennia of linguistic culture in order to express his rejection of culture.

Without the *erōs* towards truth, theology would not exist, and without the *erōs* towards the beautiful no ritual expressions would exist. Even more serious is the rejection of the *erōs* quality of love with respect to God. The consequence of this rejection is that love towards God becomes an impossible concept to be replaced by obedience to God. But obedience is not love. It can be the opposite of love. Without the desire of man to be reunited with his origin, the love towards God becomes a meaningless word.

The *erōs* quality of love is in a polar way related to what could be called the *philia* quality of love. While *erōs* represents the transpersonal pole, *philia* represents the personal pole. Neither of them is possible without the other. There is *erōs* quality in *philia*. And there is *philia* quality in *erōs*. They are in a polar way interdependent. This implies that without the radical separation of the self-centred self neither the creative nor the religious *erōs* is possible. Beings without a personal centre are without *erōs*, although they are not without *epithymia*. He who cannot relate himself as an 'I' to a 'thou' cannot relate himself to the true and the good and to the ground of being in which they are rooted. He who cannot love the friend cannot love the artistic expression of ultimate reality. Kierkegaard's stages of the aesthetical and the ethical and the religious are not stages but qualities which appear in structural interdependence. Conversely, *philia* is dependent on *erōs*. Concepts like participation and communion point to the *erōs* quality in every *philia* relation. It is the desire to unite with a power of being which is both most separated and most understandable and which radiates possibilities and realities of the good and the true in the manifestation of its incomparable individuality. But *erōs* and *philia* are not only united in the individual relation. They are also united in the communion of social groups. In families, and national groups, the desire for participation is directed towards the power of being which is embodied in the group, even if special relations of the *philia* type are lacking. The very fact that such groups consist of individuals with whom an I-thou relation is potentially given, distinguishes the *erōs* within a group from the *erōs* which is effective, e.g. in artistic creations. Love as *philia* presupposes some amount of familiarity with the object of love. For this reason Aristotle asserted that *philia* is possible only between equals. This is true if 'equal' is defined in a sufficiently large way and not in terms of an esoteric group.

As we have already indicated, *erōs* as well as *philia* contains an element of *epithymia*. This is most obvious in those cases in which a *philia* and *erōs* relation is united with sexual attraction or fulfilment. But it is true not only in these cases. It is always true. In this respect depth psychology has discovered a side of human existence which should not be covered again by idealistic or moralistic fears and postulates. The *appetitus* of every being to fulfil itself through union with other beings is universal and underlies the *erōs* as well as the *philia* quality of love. There is an element of libido even in the most spiritualized friendship and in the most ascetic mysticism. A saint without libido would cease to be a creature. But there is no such saint.

Up to this point the quality of love which dominates the New Testament, the *agapē* quality, has been disregarded. This has been done not because *agapē* is the last and highest form of love, but because *agapē* enters from another dimension into the whole of life and into all qualities of love. One could call *agapē* the depth of love or love in relation to the ground of life. One could say that in *agapē* ultimate reality manifests itself and transforms life and love. *Agapē* is love cutting into love, just as revelation is reason cutting into reason and the Word of God is the Word cutting into all words. This, however, is the subject of the last chapter.

At this point we must answer the questions raised in the first chapter about the concept of self-love. If love is the drive towards the reunion of the separated, it is hard to speak meaningfully of self-love. For within the unity of self-consciousness there is no real separation, comparable to the separation of a self-centred being from all other beings. Certainly the completely self-centred being, man, is self-centred only because his self is split into a self which is subject and a self which is object. But there is neither separation in this structure, nor the desire for reunion. Self-love is a metaphor, and it should not be treated as a concept. The lack of conceptual clarity in the concept of self-love is manifest in the fact that the term is used in three different and partly contradictory senses. It is used in the sense of natural self-affirmation (e.g. loving one's neighbour as oneself). It is used in the sense of selfishness (e.g. the desire to draw all things into oneself). It is used in the sense of self-acceptance (e.g. the affirmation of oneself in the way in which one is affirmed by God). It would be an important step towards semantic clarification if the term 'self-love' were completely removed and replaced by self-affirmation, selfishness, and self-acceptance according to the context.

III

BEING AND POWER

Being as the power of being

WE have described the function of ontology as the never-ending task of describing the texture of being-as-being or as that in which everything that is participates. However, the question arises whether one cannot say something more fundamental about being than to elaborate the categories and polarities which constitute its texture. The answer is No and Yes. The answer is No, because being cannot be defined. For in every definition being is presupposed. The answer is Yes, because being can be characterized by concepts which depend on it, but which point to it in a metaphorical way. The question as to which concepts are able to perform this function can only be answered through trials which must be tested by the power they have to make man's encounter with reality understandable. The concept I suggest for a fundamental description of being as being is one within our triad of concepts, namely the concept of power. In the discussion of the nature of ontology and the significance of the concepts of love, power, and justice for past ontologies, I have already shown that the concept of power plays an important role in the description of ultimate reality. In the Aristotelian as well as in the Augustinian tradition concepts containing the element of power are used for the sake of a fundamental characterization of being-as-being. Most conspicuous in this respect is Nietzsche's philosophy of life as will to power. In an ontological discussion of power like that in which we are engaged, it is necessary to give a short interpretation of his concept of will to power. I feel confirmed in my understanding by the profound analysis of Nietzsche's concept by Martin Heidegger in his book, *Holzwege* (*Forest Roads*). Nietzsche's 'will to power' means neither will nor power, if taken in the ordinary sense of the words. He does not speak of the psychological function called will, although the will to power may become manifest in conscious acts of man, e.g. in the self-control exercised by the commanding will. But basically the will to power in Nietzsche is, as it was in Schopenhauer, a designation of the dynamic self-affirmation of life. It is, like all concepts describing ultimate reality, both literal and metaphorical. The same is true of the meaning of power in the concept 'will to power'. It is not the sociological function of power which is meant, although sociological power is included as one of the manifestations of ontological power. Sociological power, namely the chance to carry through one's will against social resistance, is not the content of the will to power. The latter is the drive of everything living to realize itself with increasing intensity and extensity.

The will to power is not the will of men to attain power over men, but it is the self-affirmation of life in its self-transcending dynamics, overcoming internal and external resistance. This interpretation of Nietzsche's 'will to power' easily leads to a systematic ontology of power.

We started this chapter with the question: What can we say fundamentally about the nature of being? And the answer was: Nothing in terms of definition, but something in terms of metaphorical indication. And we suggested the concept of power for this purpose: Being is the power of being! Power, however, presupposes, even in the metaphorical use of the word, something over which it proves its power. We spoke of the dynamic self-affirmation of life overcoming internal and external resistance. But, we must ask, what can resist the power of being, if everything that is participates in it? Where is the ontological place of that which the power of being is able to overcome, if all possible places are established by the power of being? What can that be which tries to negate being and is negated by it? There is only one answer possible: That which is conquered by the power of being is non-being. It is an old answer, given in the myth long before the dawn of philosophy, repeated in rational terms by philosophers in all cultures and centuries, brought to a renewed attention in our time by the leading Existentialist philosophers. However, if one tries to restate this answer one must be aware that one has touched at the basic mystery of existence and that one has no chance to explain the riddle of non-being in terms which do not bear in themselves the scars of non-being, namely the language of the paradox. Nobody can fail to ask the question: How can non-being have the power to resist being? Does it not appear in such a statement as a part of being itself, and if so, is it not swallowed up into being, so that the metaphor 'power of being' becomes meaningless? It is understandable that the analytic logic of our time becomes impatient if such language is used and speaks of meaningless sentences. But if it becomes impatient with present-day ontology it must become impatient with all ontology and reject the works of almost all philosophers of past and present. And that is what logical positivists have done. But such a procedure does not defeat philosophers of the past. It defeats those who try to defeat them.

The answer to the question how non-being can resist the power of being, can only be that non-being is not foreign to being, but that it is that quality of being by which everything that participates in being is negated. Non-being is the negation of being within being itself. Each of these words is, of course, used metaphorically. But metaphorical language can be true language, pointing to something that is both revealed and hidden in this language. Being which includes non-being is finite being. 'Finite' means carrying within one's being the destiny not to be. It designates a limited power of being, limited between a beginning and an end, between non-being before and non-being after. This, however, is only a part of the answer. The other part must explain why in the balance of being and non-being, being prevails. The answer is both logical and existential. Logically (and linguistically) it is obvious that non-being is possible only as the negation of being. Being logically precedes non-being. That which is and comes to an end logically precedes the end. The negative 'lives' by the positive which it negates. But these answers, evident as they are, do not satisfy the question of the prevalence of being over non-being. Could one not speak of a balance in which neither prevails? To this only an existential answer is possible. It is what one has called the answer of faith or courage. Courage, and that in faith which is courage, affirms the ultimate prevalence of being over non-being. It affirms the presence of the infinite in everything finite. And a theology which is based on such a courage tries to show that, as non-being is dependent on the being it negates, so the awareness of finitude presupposes a place above finitude from which the finite is seen as finite. But the act in which this place is occupied is courage and not reasoning.

Every being affirms its own being. Its life is its self-affirmation—even if its self-affirmation has the form of self-surrender. Every being resists the negation against itself. The self-affirmation of a being is correlate to the power of being it embodies. It is greater in man than in animals and in some men greater than in others. A life process is the more powerful, the more non-being it can include in its self-affirmation, without being destroyed by it. The neurotic can include only a little non-being, the average man a limited amount, the creative man a large amount, God—symbolically speaking—an infinite amount. The self-affirmation of a being in spite of non-being is the expression of its power of being. Here we are at the roots of the concept of power. Power is the possibility of self-affirmation in spite of internal and external negation. It is the possibility of overcoming non-being. Human power is the possibility of man to overcome non-being infinitely.

In several places in the history of philosophy, notably in the Platonic school, degrees of being have been spoken of. This concept is difficult and highly controversial. It appears to be meaningless if being is identified with existence in time and space. There are no degrees in existing, but an either-or. If, however, being is described as the power of being, the idea of degrees of being loses its difficulty. There are, certainly, degrees in the power of being, namely in the power of taking non-being into one's own self-affirmation.

A phenomenology of power

If there are degrees in the power of being, the question arises: Where does the power of being become manifest and how can it be measured? The answer is that the power of being becomes manifest only in the process in which it actualizes its power. In this process its power appears and can be measured. Power is real only in its actualization, in the encounter with other bearers of power and in the ever-changing balance which is the result of these encounters. Life is the dynamic actualization of being. It is not a system of solutions which could be deduced from a basic vision of life. Nothing can be deduced in a life process, nothing is determined *a priori*, nothing is final except those structures which make the dynamics of life possible. Life includes continuous decisions, not necessarily conscious decisions, but decisions which occur in the encounter between power and power. Every encounter of somebody who represents a power of being with somebody else who represents another power of being leads to a decision about the amount of power embodied in each of them. These decisions cannot be deduced *a priori*. Life is tentative. Everybody and everything has chances and must take risks, because his and its power of being remains hidden if actual encounters do not reveal it.

The typical forms in which powers of being encounter each other are a fascinating subject of phenomenological descriptions: life, e.g. in a human individual, transcends itself. It pushes forward, it runs ahead, and it encounters life in another human individual which also pushes forward, or which withdraws or which stands and resists. In each case another constellation of powers is the result. One draws another power into oneself and is either strengthened or weakened by it. One throws the foreign power of being out or assimilates it completely. One transforms the resisting powers or one adapts oneself to them. One is absorbed by them and loses one's own power of being, one grows together with them and increases their and one's own power of being. These processes are going on in every moment of life, in all relations of all beings. They go on between those powers of being which we call nature, between man and nature, between man and man, between individuals and groups, between groups and groups.

In Sartre's analyses of the encounter of man with man (in his book, *L'Être et le Néant*) he shows the power struggle taking place in the accidental look of a man at another man, as well as in the most complex forms of love relations. In these examples the continuous struggle of power of being with power of being is described in a way which does not need to take into consideration hostilities, neuroses, or pacifist ideologies. It is simply a description of life processes which occur in 'heaven' as well as in 'hell.' They belong to the structure of being. This vision of life is confirmed by the work of Toynbee, *A Study of History*, where he uses a phenomenology of power-relations for the interpretation of all important historical movements. Categories such as challenge, reaction, withdrawal, return, belong to a phenomenology of encounters. And it is not only the encounter of groups with groups, it is also the encounter of groups with nature for which he develops his phenomenology of relations. In the works of the historians and depth-psychologists we find the material for a complete phenomenology of power relations.

Toynbee's example leads to an analysis of the relation of the power of being in an individual to the power of being in a group. According to the polarity of individualization and participation which characterizes being itself, everything real is an individual power of being within an embracing whole. Within the whole of power the individual can gain or lose power of being. Whether the one or the other happens is never decided *a priori*, but is a matter of continuous concrete decisions. A child, in his early years, has power of being only within the embracing power of being which is called 'family'. But at a certain moment most children have the tendency to withdraw from the family unity to themselves and their self-realization. They feel that participation in the family life means a loss of their individual power of being. So they withdraw, mostly internally, sometimes also externally. They want to increase their power of being which, they feel, is being reduced within the group. But it may happen that after a certain time they return to the family because they feel that without the power of being of the group their own power of being is severely endangered. And again, after a certain time they may realize that they have surrendered too much to the group and that this self-surrender not only weakens their own being but also that of the group to whose power they have surrendered. Again they withdraw and the conflict continues.

The problem implied in this situation is sharpened by the 'hierarchical' structure of life. The more centred a being is the more power of being is embodied in it. The completely centred, self-related and self-aware being, man, has the greatest power of being. He has a world, not only an environment, and with it infinite potentialities of self-realization. His centredness makes him the master of his world. But where there is centredness there is a hierarchical structure of power. The nearer to the centre an element is, the more it participates in the power of the whole. The ancient parable of the revolt of the members of the body against the stomach and the answer of the stomach, that without its central position all other members would starve, shows the decisive importance of the centre for the power of being for every part. Centred structures are present not only in the organic but also in the inorganic realm, notably in the atomic and subatomic elements of matter. And even the most egalitarian societies have centres of power and decision, in which the large majority of the people participate only indirectly and in degrees. These centres are strengthened in the moment in which the fullest development of power by a social group is demanded, in emergency situations. The need for an acting centre makes even an egalitarian group hierarchical.

The centre of power is only the centre of the whole as long as it does not degrade its own centrality by using it for particular purposes. In the moment in which the representatives of the centre use the power of the whole for their particular self-realization they cease to be the actual centre, and the whole being, without a centre, disintegrates. Certainly, it is possible for a ruling group to force its will upon the whole, even if its will is not the expression of the whole. But this is possible only for a limited time. Finally, the loss of the power of the whole, through internal or external causes, is unavoidable.

Power and compulsion

This leads to the all-decisive question of the relation of power to force and compulsion. As shown in our first lecture, the confusion of these concepts has prevented a meaningful doctrine of power, especially in the social and political field. Our understanding of power as the power of being is the first step in removing this inhibition. But more is needed, because the disturbing question must be answered whether there is power without force and compulsion. If this question had to be answered negatively, would that not mean that the equation of power with compulsion is not confusion but realism?

The term 'force' points both to the strength a thing has in itself and to the way in which it has effects on other things. It forces them into a movement or behaviour without using their own active support. Of course, no thing can be forced into something which contradicts its nature. If this is attempted, the thing in question is destroyed and, perhaps, remade into something else. In this sense there is an ultimate limit to any application of force. That which is forced must preserve its identity. Otherwise it is not forced but destroyed. In the realm of physics things are forced to move or to behave in a way which is determined by their own potentialities and by the force effective upon them. The result is calculable and represents a balance of the different powers which are working in the direction of the result.

In the realm of living beings the same possibilities and the same limits of force are given. But there is a difference from the inorganic realm. As long as a living being is not transformed into a mechanism it reacts spontaneously, supporting or resisting the forces working on it. And one cannot transform a living being into a complete mechanism, without removing its centre and this means without destroying it as a living unity. One can mechanize most of its reactions, but there are always sub-centres which react spontaneously as long as the being is alive and not transferred into the realm of merely chemical processes as they occur in dead bodies. Spontaneity means that a reaction is elicited but not forced by a stimulus and consequently that it is not calculable. For a 'holistic' reaction always works through the centre, which is not calculable, because it is indivisible, constituting an individual being.

To the degree to which force in living beings needs the support of spontaneity, one could speak more adequately of compulsion or coercion. This is certainly necessary in the encounters between human beings. For in these words, 'compulsion' or 'coercion', a psychological resistance is indicated which must be overcome. And this is what power has to do if dealing with men.

Power actualizes itself through force and compulsion. But power is neither the one nor the other. It is being, actualizing itself over against the threat of non-being. It uses and abuses compulsion in order to overcome this threat. It uses and abuses force in order to actualize itself. But it is neither the one nor the other.

Therefore the question of power and compulsion must be answered in the following way: Power needs compulsion. But its use of compulsion is only effective if it is an expression of the actual power relation. If compulsion trespasses this limit it becomes self-defying and undercuts the power which it is supposed to preserve. It is not compulsion which is bad, but a compulsion which does not express the power of being in the name of which it is applied. Power needs compulsion, but compulsion needs the criterion which is implied in the actual power relation. The social and political consequences of this analysis will be developed later.

The ontological unity of love and power

If in every actualization of power compulsion is implied, how can power be united with love? All those who want to remove power for the sake of love ask this question, implying a negative answer. If power needs force and compulsion for its actualization, does it exclude love?

The ontological answer to this most urgent practical question follows from our analyses of love and power. The power of being is its possibility to affirm itself against the non-being within it and against it. The power of a being is the greater the more non-being is taken into its self-affirmation. The power of being is not dead identity but the dynamic process in which it separates itself from itself and returns to itself. The more conquered separation there is the more power there is. The process in which the separated is reunited is love.

The more reuniting love there is, the more conquered non-being there is, the more power of being there is. Love is the foundation, not the negation, of power. Whether one says that being has non-being in itself or whether one says that being separates itself from itself and reunites itself with itself, does not make any difference. The basic formula of power and the basic formula of love are identical: Separation and Reunion or Being taking Non-Being into itself.

From this ultimate unity of power and love the question can be answered: How can the compulsory element of power be united with love? Nobody felt the weight of this question more than Luther, who had to combine his highly spiritual ethics of love with his highly realistic politics of absolutistic power. Luther answered with the statement that compulsion is the strange work of love. Sweetness, self-surrender and mercy are, according to him, the proper work of love, bitterness, killing, and condemnation are its strange work, but both are works of love. What he meant could be expressed in the statement that it is the strange work of love to destroy what is against love. This, however, presupposes the unity of love and power. Love, in order to exercise its proper works, namely charity and forgiveness, must provide for a place on which this can be done, through its strange work of judging and punishing. In order to destroy what is against love, love must be united with power, and not only with power, but also with compulsory power.

This latter demand posits a new question: If love is united with the compulsory element of power, where are the limits of this union? Where does compulsion conflict with love? It conflicts with love when it prevents the aim of love, namely the reunion of the separated. Love, through compulsory power, must destroy what is against love. But love cannot destroy him who acts against love. Even when destroying his work it does not destroy him. It tries to save and fulfil him by destroying in him what is against love. The criterion is: Everything that makes reunion impossible is against love. We read that in the Middle Ages, during the trial and execution of a mass murderer, the relatives of the murdered ones fell on their knees and prayed for his soul. The destruction of his bodily existence was not felt as a negation, but as an affirmation of love. It made the reunion of the radically separated soul of the criminal with himself and with the souls of his natural enemies possible. The opposite story is that of present-day totalitarian forms of the exercise of power, in which the victims are transformed into things by fatigue, drugs, and other means and nobody, not even relatives and friends, are allowed to participate in their destruction, which is intended as a destruction of their whole being without reuniting love.

Perhaps there is one point which Luther has not seen clearly enough, namely that love's strange work, the compulsory element of power, is not only the strange but also the tragic aspect of love. It represents a price which must be paid for the reunion of the separated. And beyond this, Luther certainly has not emphasized sufficiently that love's strange work can be used by those in power as a means, not for reuniting the estranged, but for keeping themselves in power. The question, how this distortion of the doctrine of love's strange work can be prohibited, has not been asked by him. Therefore he has often been accused of a Machiavellian cynicism with respect to power. This is certainly, subjectively speaking, wrong. But it is not completely wrong with respect to the consequences of Luther's doctrine.

The question is: If love and power are united and if compulsion is inescapable in every actualization of power, how can love be united with power? The answer is the subject of the chapter on the ontology of justice.

We have discussed the term 'self-love' and have suggested its complete removal. One does not speak of self-power, but one uses the term 'self-control' in the sense of power over oneself. Again we ask: Does the structure of self-relatedness admit something like power of the self over the self? The question must be decided in the same way as it has been decided in the case of self-love. The term is metaphorical. There is no self which fights against another self, with which, on the other hand, it is identical. The power of the self is its self-centredness. Self-control is the preservation of this centredness against disruptive tendencies, coming from the elements which constitute the centre: One could say that a struggle is going on between these elements, each of them trying to determine the centre. But such a struggle presupposes that there is a centred self within which the conflict of drives can occur. The centre precedes logically every element which tries to determine it. Power over oneself is the power of the self over the forces which constitute it and each of which tries to determine it. We must, however, ask: How can a centre (a symbol taken from geometry) have power besides the power of the elements of which it is the centre? The answer is, that it has not such independent power but that its power is the power of a stabilized balance of the elements which are centred in it. The stabilized balance of its constitutive elements is the power of the centre. In this balance some elements prevail, others are subordinated but not ineffective. Self-control is the activity of the centred self in preserving and strengthening the established balance against disruptive tendencies. This can be done by the exclusion from the centre of many elements which are present in the self. It also can be done by a union of many elements in the centre without the exclusion of most of them. Whether self-control is exercised in the former or in the latter way decides about the ethical meaning of self-control, the former way for a more puritan, the latter for a more romantic ethics. But the basic structure is the same in both cases: self-centredness implies the power which the self exercises through a stable balance of its constituent elements over each of these elements. In this sense every self is a power structure.

IV

BEING AND JUSTICE

Justice as the form of being

ACTUALIZED being or life unites dynamics with form. Everything real has a form, be it an atom, be it the human mind. That which has no form has no being. At the same time, everything real drives beyond itself. It is not satisfied with the form in which it finds itself. It urges towards a more embracing, ultimately to *the* all-embracing form. Everything wants to grow. It wants to increase its power of being in forms which include and conquer more non-being. Metaphorically speaking, one could say that the molecule wants to become a crystal, the crystal a cell, the cell a centre of cells, the plant animal, the animal man, the man god, the weak strong, the isolated participating, the imperfect perfect, and so on! In this drive it can happen that a being, when transcending itself loses itself. It can happen that it destroys its given form without attaining a new form, thus annihilating itself. Life meets this threat by creating forms of growth. The self-transcendence of a being occurs in forms which determine the process of self-transcendence. But this determination is never complete. If it were, one could not speak of self-transcendence. One would have to speak of self-expression. The incompleteness of the laws of growth produces a risk in everything living. In transcending itself a being may fulfil and it may destroy itself. One could call this the risk of creativity. Symbolically, one could say that even God, in creating, took the risk upon Himself that creation would turn into destruction.

In the vision in which Parmenides receives the answer to the philosophical question, it is *dikē*, the goddess of justice, who introduces him into the truth about being. Justice is not a social category far removed from ontological inquiries, but it is a category without which no ontology is possible. In the poetic fragment of Parmenides we have an archaic ontology of justice. Heraclitus, in his words about the *logos*, the law which determines the movement of the *kosmos*, applies the concept of the *logos* both to the laws of nature and to the laws of the city. According to Plato, justice is the uniting function in the individual man and in the social group. It is the embracing form in both cases. Their power of being depends on it. In Stoicism it is the same *logos* which works as physical law in nature and as moral law in the human mind. It judges as principle of justice all positive laws. It gave the Roman Stoics criteria for the formulation and administration of the Roman law. It was seen in its absolute, cosmic validity, whatever the consequences of its execution may be. Whenever the ontological foundation of justice was removed, and a positivistic interpretation of law was tried, no criteria against arbitrary tyranny or utilitarian relativism were left. In the fight of Socrates with the Sophists this was the decisive point. In the defence of the 'rights of man' against cynicism and dictatorship, the same fight is going on to-day. It can be won only by a new foundation of natural law and justice. A glimpse at the Old Testament shows that in spite of the unmetaphysical character of prophetic thinking, the principle of justice they pronounce governs not only Israel, but also mankind and nature. In later Judaism the law is hypostasized in the eternal realm. Only its manifestation is temporal. This implies that it is the form of being which is valid for everything in every period. Obedience to it gives power of being. Disobedience involves self-destruction.

If justice is the form in which the power of being actualizes itself, justice must be adequate to the dynamics of power (as discussed before). It must be able to give form to the encounters of being with being. The problem of 'justice in encounter' is given with the fact that it is impossible to say before the encounter happens how the power relation will be within the encounter. Many possibilities are given in every moment. Each of these possibilities demands a special form. A wrong, unjust, power relation may destroy life. In every act of justice daring is necessary and risk is unavoidable. There are no principles which could be applied mechanically and which would guarantee that justice is done.

Nevertheless there are principles of justice expressing the form of being in its universal and unchanging character.

Principles of justice

On the basis of an ontology of love it is obvious that love is the principle of justice. If life as the actuality of being is essentially the drive towards the reunion of the separated, it follows that the justice of being is the form which is adequate to this movement. The further principles to be derived from the basic principle mediate between it and the concrete situation in which the risk of justice is demanded. There are four principles which perform this mediation.

The first principle is that of adequacy, namely the adequacy of the form to the content. There is a complaint, as old as human laws, that laws which were adequate in the past are still in force, although inadequate in the present. They do not give the form in which creative encounters of power with power are possible and a definite power of being results. They prevent such encounters from becoming creative, or, in terms of the ontology of love, from reuniting the separated. Laws, governing the family structure of another period or its economic relations, may destroy families and disrupt the class unity of this period. The possibility for such discrepancies between law and actual encounter is based on the fact that the forms which once expressed the power of being, have a tendency towards self-continuation beyond the point of their adequacy. This is so even in nature, as the remnants of former biological stages in later stages of development show. It is confirmed by the conservatism of institutions in man's cultural and social existence. In both cases it is the risk of self-transcendence which keeps life in the bondage of tested institutions. But the price paid for the safety in the old form is paid in terms of injustice. And injustice in terms of the inadequacy of the form ultimately undermines safety, so that the price was paid in vain.

The second principle of justice is that of equality. It is implicit in every law, in so far as the law is equally valid for the equals. But the question is: Who are the equals? In what sense is equality meant? In Plato's *Republic*, the central concern of which is the idea of justice, a large group of human beings, i.e. the slaves, are excluded from full humanity and the corresponding justice. Amongst the three groups who are equals as citizens and as such fully human, great inequalities do exist with respect to their claims for distributive justice. Christianity has reduced the fundamental inequality of the ancient world, namely that between human beings with full humanity and those with limited humanity. There is ultimate equality between all men in the view of God and His justice is equally offered to all of them. Hierarchy and aristocracy are irrelevant for the ultimate relation. But they are very relevant for the inner human relations. Slavery was not abolished in the early Church and the medieval order was feudal, establishing qualifications of justice according to the claim for justice of each grade of social standing. The principle of equality was restricted to the equals within the same ontological degree, inside and outside the human society. Justice is based on a cosmic hierarchy. It is the form in which this hierarchy actualizes itself.

The principle of equality can be understood in the opposite way. It can be applied democratically to every human being. If this is done, one points to the possession of reason in everyone who deserves the name 'man'. It is their potential rationality which makes all men equal. This potentiality must be actualized if real equality is to be created. But in the process of actualization innumerable differences appear, differences in the given nature of the individual, differences in his given social opportunity, differences in his given creativity, differences in all sides of his power of being. These differences entail differences in his social power and consequently in his claim for distributive justice. But these differences are functional and not ontological, as in the systems of hierarchical thinking. They are not unchangeable. Nevertheless they prevent an egalitarian system of society. Actually there is no egalitarian structure in any society.

The relation of equality and justice depends on the

power of being in a man and his corresponding intrinsic claim for justice. The definition of this claim is rather diverse. It is one thing if he is posited on a grade of a hierarchical stairway and he expects to receive the justice which fits his grade. It is another if he is considered a unique and incomparable individual and he expects a special justice which is adapted to his particular power of being. It is still another if he is considered a potential bearer of reason and he expects the justice which is claimed by his dignity as a rational being in different states of development. In all these cases equality is present, but a qualified equality, never an egalitarian one. Every solution of the problem of man's freedom can be accepted in the context of the present discussion. What is decisive is only that man is considered as a deliberating, deciding, responsible person. Therefore one had probably better speak of the principle of personality as a principle of justice. The content of this principle is the demand to treat every person as a person. Justice is always violated if men are dealt with as if they were things. This has been called 'reification' (*Verdinglichung*) or 'objectivation' (*Vergegenständlichung*). In any case it contradicts the justice of being, the intrinsic claim of every person to be considered a person. This claim includes and circumscribes the relation of freedom to justice. Freedom can mean the inner superiority of the person over enslaving conditions in the external world. The Stoic slave and the Christian slave were equal in their independence of the social conditions which contradicted external freedom but which were not necessarily in conflict with their spiritual freedom, with their persons and with their claim to be considered as persons. The Stoic participates in the justice of the universe and its rational structure; the Christian expects the justice of the Kingdom of God. An enslavement of the personal centre is not implied in one's social destiny. Spiritual freedom is possible even 'in chains'. In contrast to this ideal of non-political spiritual freedom, liberalism tries to remove the enslaving conditions. The transition from the one to the other idea of freedom is the awareness that there are social conditions which prevent spiritual freedom either generally or for the great majority of people. This was the argument of the revolutionary Anabaptists in the Reformation period. It was the argument of many social reformers in all periods of Christianity, and it was the argument of humanistic and religious socialists in our time. But more than this is involved in the liberal fight for political freedom. 'Liberty' is considered to be an essential principle of justice because the freedom of political and cultural self-determination is seen as an essential element of personal existence. Slavery in all forms contradicts justice even if both the master and the slave can participate in transcendent freedom. This liberal doctrine of justice is an exception in the total history of mankind, and it is today receding in influence. Does our ontological analysis give an answer to the question of freedom in liberalism? And is there an answer to the previous question of the aristocratic and the democratic idea of equality in connexion with it?

The ontology of love gives the answer. If justice is the form of the reunion of the separated, it must include both the separation without which there is no love and the reunion in which love is actualized. This is the reason why frequently the principle of fraternity or solidarity or comradeship or, more adequately, community has been added to the principles of equality and liberty. This addition has, however, been rejected in the name of a formal concept of justice, and under the assumption that community is an emotional principle adding nothing essential to the rational concept of justice—on the contrary, endangering its strictness. The decision of all these interwoven problems is dependent on the two remaining subjects of this chapter: the qualities of justice and the relationship of justice to power and love.

Levels of justice

We spoke several times about distributive justice, a concept taken from Aristotle, who distinguishes it from retributive justice. In order to discuss this distinction we must see it within the larger context in which the different levels of justice appear.

The basis of justice is the intrinsic claim for justice of everything that has being. The intrinsic claim of a tree is different from the intrinsic claim of a person. The claims for justice based on the different forms in which the power of being actualizes itself are different. But they are just claims if they are adequate to the power of being on which they are based. Justice is first of all a claim raised silently or vocally by a being on the basis of its power of being. It is an intrinsic claim, expressing the form in which a thing or a person is actualized. If this claim is uttered by him who makes it, it may be adequate to his intrinsic claim or it may not be. Whether oneself or others give voice to one's intrinsic claim for justice, the voice can be just and it can be unjust. One of the injustices in the transformation of the intrinsic claim for justice into practical judgements is the suppression of the dynamic element in the actualization of being. The opposite injustice is the denial of the static structure within which the dynamic element can be effective.

The second form of justice is the tributive or proportional justice. It appears as distributive, attributive, retributive justice, giving to everything proportionally to what it deserves, positively or negatively. It is a calculating justice, measuring the power of being of all things in terms of what shall be given to them or of what shall be withheld from them. I have called this form of justice tributive because it decides about the tribute a thing or a person ought to receive according to his special powers of being. Tribute is given by conquered nations to the rulers of the victorious nations. It is given to outstanding persons or groups by grateful adherents. It is given to representatives of power as a symbol of the acknowledgement of their function by those who are subject to their power. Attributive justice attributes to beings what they are and can claim to be. Distributive justice gives to any being the proportion of goods which is due to him; retributive justice does the same, but in negative terms, in terms of deprivation of goods or active punishment. This latter consideration makes it clear that there is no essential difference between distributive and retributive justice. Both of them are proportional and can be measured in quantitative terms. In the realm of law and law-enforcement the tributive form of justice is the norm. But there are some exceptions, and they point to a third form of justice.

I suggest that this third form be called transforming or creative justice. It is based on the fact to which I have already referred that the intrinsic justice is dynamic. As such it cannot be defined in definite terms, and therefore the tributive justice is never adequate to it because it calculates in fixed proportions. One never knows *a priori* what the outcome of an encounter of power with power will be. If one judges such an encounter and its outcome according to previous power proportions, one is necessarily unjust, even if one is legally right. Examples of this situation are a matter of daily experience. They include all trespasses of the positive law in the name of a superior law which is not yet formulated and valid. They include struggles for power which are in conflict with indefinite or obsolete rules, and the outcome of which is an increase in the power of being in both the victor and the conquered. They include all those events in which justice demands the resignation of justice, an act without which no human relation and no human group could last. More exactly one should speak of the resignation of proportional justice for the sake of creative justice. What is the criterion of creative justice? In order to answer this question one must ask which is the ultimate intrinsic claim for justice in a being? The answer is: Fulfilment within the unity of universal fulfilment. The religious symbol for this is the kingdom of God.

The classical expression of the third form of justice is given in the Biblical literature of both Testaments. It is not quite right to say that justice in the Bible is the negation of proportional justice. There are innumerable places in both Testaments where the symbol of the judge is applied to God or the Christ; and there are other places where the injustice of human judges is exposed and more seriously condemned than almost any other sin. Nevertheless, the main emphasis goes in another direction. The *zadikim*, the just ones, are those who subject themselves to the divine orders according to which everything in nature and history is created and moves. But this subjection is not the acceptance of commandments as such, but it is the loving obedience to him who is the source of the law. Therefore, the concept of the *zadik* unites subjection to the law with piety towards him who gives the law. Under the personalistic terminology of the Old Testament a profound awareness of the ontological character of the law is hidden. In later Judaism it came into the open and helped to prepare the ontological interpretation of Christ as the Logos in the early Church. As in its application to man, so in its application to God justice means more than proportional justice. It means creative justice and is expressed in the divine grace which forgives in order to reunite. God is not bound to the given proportion between merit and tribute. He can creatively change the proportion, and does it in order to fulfil those who according to proportional justice would be excluded from fulfilment. Therefore the divine justice can appear as plain injustice. In the paradox of the 'justification by grace through faith', as stated by Paul, the divine justice is manifest in the divine act which justifies him who is unjust. This, like every act of forgiveness, can only be understood through the idea of creative justice. And creative justice is the form of reuniting love.

The ontological unity of justice, power, and love

Justice was defined as the form in which power of being actualizes itself in the encounter of power with power. Justice is immanent in power, since there is no power of being without its adequate form. But whenever power of being encounters power of being, compulsion cannot be avoided. The question then is: What is the relation of justice to the compulsory element of power? The answer must be: it is not compulsion which is unjust, but a compulsion which destroys the object of compulsion instead of working towards its fulfilment. If the totalitarian State dehumanizes those for the sake of whom it enforces its laws, their power of being as persons is dissolved and their intrinsic claim is denied. It is not compulsion which violates justice, but a compulsion which disregards the intrinsic claim of a being to be acknowledged as what it is within the context of all beings. It may well be that a compulsion which prevents the punishment of a law-breaker destroys his power of being and violates his claim to be reduced in his power of being according to proportional justice. This is the truth in Hegel's formula that the criminal has a right to punishment. A power structure in which compulsion works against the intrinsic justice of its elements is not strengthened but weakened. The unacknowledged, justified claims, although suppressed, do not disappear. They are effective against the whole in which they are suppressed and they may ultimately destroy a power structure which is neither able to accept them as participants, nor able to throw them out as strange bodies. The intrinsic claim in everything that is cannot be violated without violating the violator. This is equally true of biological, psychological, and of sociological structures of power. The mental power of a human being, e.g., can express itself in three forms. It can suppress elements which belong to it, as special desires or hopes or ideas. In this case the suppressed elements remain and turn the mind against itself, driving it towards disintegration. Or the mental power of a human being can receive resisting elements which belong to it, elevating them into unity with the whole. Or the mental power can throw them out radically as foreign bodies whose claim to belong to the whole is successfully rejected. In the second and the third case the human mind exercises justice in opposite directions towards the resisting elements. In the first case it violates the intrinsic claim of a being and endangers itself. This psychological example is also valid for biological and sociological structures of power and will be discussed in one of the following chapters.

As in power, justice is immanent in love. A love of any type, and love as a whole if it does not include justice, is chaotic self-surrender, destroying him who loves as well as him who accepts such love. Love is the drive for reunion of the separated. It presupposes that there is something to be reunited, something relatively independent that stands upon itself. Sometimes the love of complete self-surrender has been praised and called the fulfilment of love. But the question is: What kind of self-surrender is it and what is it that it surrenders? If a self whose power of being is weakened or vanishing surrenders, his surrender is worth nothing. He is a self which has not received from himself the justice to which he is entitled, according to his intrinsic claim for justice. The surrender of such an emaciated self is not genuine love because it extinguishes and does not unite what is estranged. The love of this kind is the desire to annihilate one's responsible and creative self for the sake of the participation in another self which by the assumed act of love is made responsible for himself and oneself. The chaotic self-surrender does not give justice to the other one, because he who surrenders did not give justice to himself. It is justice to oneself to affirm one's own power of being and to accept the claim for justice which is implied in this power. Without this justice there is no reuniting love, because there is nothing to unite.

This leads to the question of justice towards oneself, a question which is analogous to the questions of self-love and self-control. In both cases we spoke of a metaphorical use of the term. We must do so also in the case of justice towards oneself. There is no independent self which could decide about the claim for justice by another self with which it happens to be identical. But there is a definite sense in which one can speak of justice towards oneself, namely in the sense that the deciding centre is just towards the elements of which it is the centre. Justice towards oneself in this sense decides, e.g. that the puritan form of self-control is unjust because it excludes elements of the self which have a just claim to be admitted to the general balance of strivings. Repression is injustice against oneself, and it has the consequence of all injustice: it is self-destructive because of the resistance of the elements which are excluded. This, however, does not mean that the chaotic admittance of all strivings to the central decision is a demand of the justice towards oneself. It may be highly unjust, in so far as it makes a balanced centre impossible and dissolves the self into a process of disconnected impulses. This is the danger of the romantic or open type of self-control. It can become as unjust towards oneself as the puritan or closed type of self-control. To be just towards oneself means to actualize as many potentialities as possible without losing oneself in disruption and chaos.

This is a warning not to be unjust towards oneself in the relation of love. For this is always also an injustice towards him who accepts the injustice which we exercise towards ourselves. He is prevented from being just because he is forced to abuse by being abused.

Love does not do more than justice demands, but love is the ultimate principle of justice. Love reunites; justice preserves what is to be united. It is the form in which and through which love performs its work. Justice in its ultimate meaning is creative justice, and creative justice is the form of reuniting love.

V

THE UNITY OF JUSTICE, LOVE, AND POWER IN PERSONAL RELATIONS

Ontology and ethics

IN the first four chapters I have tried to lay the ontological foundations on which the ethical structures discussed in the last three chapters are supposed to be built. But this analogy, taken from architecture, is only partly adequate. There is no real separation between substructure and superstructure: One cannot discuss the ontological foundations of love, power, and justice without presupposing their ethical functions, and one cannot discuss their ethical functions without referring constantly to their ontological foundations.

Ethics is the science of man's moral existence, asking for the roots of the moral imperative, the criteria of its validity, the sources of its contents, the forces of its realization. The answer to each of these questions is directly or indirectly dependent on a doctrine of being. The roots of the moral imperative, the criteria of its validity, the sources of its contents, the forces of its realization, all this can be elaborated only in terms of an analysis of man's being and universal being. There is no answer in ethics without an explicit or implicit assertion about the nature of being.

The most important attempt to make ethics independent of ontology was the philosophy of values. But if ever a philosophy was dated, it was the theory of values as it appeared before the middle of the nineteenth century. The reasons for its appearance and its dominating position are obvious. After the so-called breakdown of classical German philosophy, especially of Hegel's system, the interpretation of nature and man was delivered into the hands of a mechanistic science and a materialistic ontology. Ethics was considered as a problem in biology, psychology, and sociology. Every 'ought-to-be' was transformed into an 'is', every norm into a fact, every idea into an ideology. In this situation responsible philosophers looked for a way of giving philosophical validity to those elements in reality on which human dignity and the meaning of existence depend. They found the way which was called the doctrine of values. Values, they argued, practical as well as theoretical, have a standing of their own. They are not dependent on the order of being, as understood by naturalism. Since the ontology of their time was materialistic they rejected any attempt to give an ontological foundation to the realm of value. The good, the beautiful, the true are beyond being. They have the character of 'ought to be'. but not of 'is'. This was an ingenious way to save the validity of ethical norms, without interfering with reality as seen by reductionist naturalism. But the way was blocked from both sides. From the side of science the allied forces of biology, psychology, and sociology refused to set the values free from the hold they had upon them, and believed themselves to have with scientific right. They tried to prove that biological, psychological, and sociological laws are sufficient to explain the establishment of values, individually as well as socially. Values, they concluded, are valuations. Not their validity, but their rise, growth, and fall, must be explained. The deeper they dug into the dynamics of life, the more evidence for their thesis was collected. The safety gap between being and value seemed to disappear. Values are expressions of existence unable to judge existence from a place beyond it. The resistance of value-philosophy against this threat became increasingly weaker.

But even more decisive was the attack from the opposite side, namely an analysis of the nature of values itself. Values demand to be actualized in existence and through existence. The question then arises: How is this possible, if there is no ontological participation of values in existence, but an unbridgeable gap between them? How can a commandment coming from beyond existence have any influence on existence? This question is completely unanswerable if existence is described in terms of mechanical necessity. But even if freedom is affirmed (an ontological interference with scientific determinism for the sake of the value theory) the question remains: How can commandments coming from beyond existence possess obligation for existing beings with whose being they have no essential relationship? Again the value theory was unable to answer. These questions could not be silenced any longer: What is the ontological foundation for values? How are what have been called values rooted in being itself? And even more, is it meaningful to maintain the value theory at all? Is it not more adequate to inquire into the structures of reality on which ethics are based? In other words, does not the value theory itself demand that it be replaced by ontology?

But even if one accepts this criticism of the value theory, one may try to escape the ontological alternative by suggesting other alternatives. The first of them is the pragmatic one. Ethical norms, pragmatism argues, are the objectivation of human experiences. They establish rules describing the pragmatically most adequate behaviour. But one asks immediately: Adequate to what? Every situation is ambiguous in its ethical aspect and admits different answers to the question of adequacy. The pragmatic escape from ontology (conscious ontology, for an unconscious ontology is always present) is barred by the question of the criteria of pragmatic adequacy. The second, somehow opposite alternative is the theological one. Ethical norms are given by God. This is the basis of their validity. This solution seems to account for that quality of ethical experience for which neither pragmatism nor value theory have an explanation, the unconditional character of the moral imperative. But does the theological alternative avoid ontology? There are two possibilities of interpreting it: The one I would call heteronomous, the other I would call theonomous. The first understands the moral commandments as expressions of a divine will, which is sovereign and without criteria. It cannot be measured in terms of adequacy to human nature. It must be obeyed as it is given through revelation. But the question then is: Why should anyone obey the commandments of this divine lawgiver? How are they distinguished from commands given by a human tyrant? He is stronger than I am. He can destroy me. But is not that destruction more to be feared which would follow the submission of one's personality centre to a strange will? Would not this be just the denial of the moral imperative? The other way of the theological foundation of the moral imperative is the theonomous one. It avoids the destructiveness of the heteronomous way. But just for this reason it becomes ontological. It asserts (in agreement with the predominant trend of classical theology) that the law given by God is man's essential nature, put against him as law. If man were not estranged from himself, if his essential nature were not distorted in his actual existence, no law would stand against him. The law is not strange to man. It is natural law. It represents his true nature from which he is estranged. Every valid ethical commandment is an expression of man's essential relation to himself, to others and to the universe. This alone makes it obligatory and its denial self-destructive. This alone accounts for the unconditional form of the moral imperative, however questionable and conditioned the contents may be. The theonomous solution leads inescapably to ontological problems. If God is not seen as a strange and arbitrary lawgiver, if His authority is not heteronomous but theonomous, ontological presuppositions are accepted. Theonomous ethics include ontology. And they also verify the ontological foundations on which they rest. The ontological statements about the nature of love, power, and justice are verified if they are able to solve the otherwise insoluble problems of the ethics of love, power, and justice. To show that this is the case we must consider the ethical functions of love, power, and justice in the spheres of personal relations, of social institutions and of the holy. In the first sphere, justice is leading, in the second sphere, power, and in the third sphere, love. But all three principles are effective in each sphere. And the sphere of the holy is a quality in the other spheres, and only in some respects a sphere of its own. So we shall speak first of justice, love, and power in human relations, then of power, justice, and love in social institutions, then of love, power, and justice in relation to the holy.

Justice in personal encounters

Man becomes man in personal encounters. Only by meeting a 'thou' does man realize that he is an 'ego'. No natural object within the whole universe can do this to him. Man can transcend himself in all directions in knowledge and control. He can use everything for his purposes. He is limited only by his finitude. But these limits can be reduced infinitely. Nobody can say where the final limits of human power lie. In his encounter with the universe, man is able to transcend any imaginable limit. But there is a limit for man which is definite and which he always encounters, the other man. The other one, the 'thou', is like a wall which cannot be removed or penetrated or used. He who tries to do so, destroys himself. The 'thou' demands by his very existence to be acknowledged as a 'thou' for an 'ego' and as an 'ego' for himself. This is the claim which is implied in his being. Man can refuse to listen to the intrinsic claim of the other one. He can disregard his demand for justice. He can remove or use him. He can try to transform him into a manageable object, a thing, a tool. But in doing so he meets the resistance of him who has the claim to be acknowledged as an ego. And this resistance forces him either to meet the other one as an ego or to give up his own ego-quality. Injustice against the other one is always injustice against oneself. The master who treats the slave not as an ego but as a thing endangers his own quality as an ego. The slave by his very existence hurts the master as much as he is hurt by him. The external inequality is balanced by the destruction of the ego-quality of the master.

This leads to the question whether the 'Golden Rule' can be considered as the principle of justice in personal encounters. It is used even by Jesus. And it is certainly an expression of practical wisdom to do to people what one wants to have done by them! But it is not the criterion of justice in personal encounters. For it may well be that one wants to receive benefits which contradict the justice towards oneself and which would contradict equally the justice towards the other one, if he received them. They are unjust if given and unjust if received. We should reject them if we are asked for them. This is comparatively easy if things are demanded or given that are obviously evil. But it is difficult if we feel obliged to fulfil what seems to be a just claim, a claim we ourselves would make. Nevertheless we hesitate. We are suspicious of the others as we would be of ourselves; we suspect that behind the manifest meaning of the demand something else is hidden that should be rejected, an unconscious hostility, the desire to dominate, the will to exploit, the instinct of self-destruction. In all these cases the justice in a person-to-person encounter cannot be defined in terms of the 'Golden Rule'.

We have discovered the absolutely valid formal principle of justice in every personal encounter, namely the acknowledgement of the other person as a person. But we have tried in vain to derive contents for this formal principle from the 'Golden Rule'. The question then is: Are there other ways to discover such contents? A seemingly incontestable answer is: The cultural process gives the contents; they are provided by human experience, embodied in laws, tradition, authorities as well as the individual conscience. He who follows those rules and decides under the guidance of his conscience, has a solid foundation for justice in personal encounters. Mankind is never without a treasury of ethical wisdom which prevents its self-destruction and which, in religious terminology, is based on universal revelation. Since justice is the form of the power of being, the being of mankind could not have lasted for one moment without structures of justice in the encounter of man with man. Most of the daily encounters between human beings are determined by these sources of justice. In some cases law, tradition, and authority are predominant, in others the individual conscience. This is an important difference and can lead to tragic conflicts, as classically described in Sophocles' *Antigone*. But it is not decisive for our problems. For objective rules and individual conscience are interdependent. Laws, traditions, and authorities have been established as sources of justice through decisions in which the individual conscience was involved. And on the other hand, the individual conscience has been shaped by processes in which laws, traditions, and authorities have been internalized, and have become rules of justice which make external compulsion unnecessary. In a somehow paradoxical way one could say: Law is externalized conscience; conscience is internalized law. Rules of justice are created by the interplay of law and conscience.

Is it possible to transcend this situation? Is there a way, other than the interplay of law and conscience, to get contents for the justice of person-to-person encounter? The only answer left is the classical theory of natural law, the belief that it is possible to discover structures of human relations which are universally, unchangeably, and concretely valid. The Ten Commandments are considered by classical theology as statements of the natural law and so are their interpretations in the Sermon on the Mount. The Roman Church adds the ecclesiastical interpretation of both. It does not deny that they are natural laws. But because awareness of them is ineffective and distorted, the Church must restate them. But they remain natural law and they are, in principle, rationally recognizable. In our analysis of equality and freedom, two basic tenets of the natural law theory, we have tried to show that in the moment in which these principles are used for concrete decisions they become indefinite, changing, relative. This holds true of all contents of the natural law. They are like the principles which are supposed to control the sexual relations—historically conditioned and often in flagrant conflict with the intrinsic justice of these relations. The natural law theory cannot answer the questions of the contents of justice. And it is possible to show that this question cannot be answered at all in terms of justice alone. The question of the content of justice drives to the principles of love and power.

The unity of justice and love in personal encounters

Justice as proportional justice cannot fulfil the quest implied in a concrete situation, but love can. One should never say that love's work starts where the work of justice ends. For love shows what is just in the concrete situation. Nothing is more false than to say to somebody: since I love you and you love me, I don't need to get justice from you or you from me, for love eliminates the need for justice. Such language is used by people who want to avoid the obligations which are connected with justice. It is said by tyrannical rulers to their subjects and by tyrannical parents to their children. And even if they do not say it, they act accordingly. It is a clever way of trying to escape the responsibility and the self-restriction demanded by justice. Often, the love which supposedly transcends justice is nothing more than an emotional outburst of self-surrender, alternating with emotional outbursts of hostility.

Therefore it is false to say: Love gives what justice cannot give; love drives to a self-surrender which is beyond the demand of justice. There is much self-surrender which is the demand of proportional justice, e.g. death for a cause on which one's own existence depends. But there are other kinds of self-surrender which are not demanded by proportional justice. They are demanded by love. However, if they are demanded by love they are demanded by creative justice. For the creative element in justice is love.

Love, in this respect, has the same relation to justice which revelation has to reason. And this is not an accidental analogy. It is rooted in the nature of both revelation and love. Both of them transcend the rational norm without destroying it. Both of them have an 'ecstatic element'. Love in some of its expressions, e.g. in those which Paul gives in 1 Cor. xiii can be called justice in ecstasy, as revelation can be called reason in ecstasy. This also is confirmed by Paul when he derives both revelatory experiences and the working of love from the divine spirit. And as revelation does not give additional information in the realm where cognitive reason decides, so love does not drive to additional acts in the realm where practical reason decides. Both give another dimension to reason, revelation to cognitive reason, love to practical reason. Neither of them denies that to which it gives the dimensions of depth, namely to reason. As revelation does not contradict the structures of cognitive reason (otherwise revelation could not be received), so love does not contradict justice (otherwise it could not be actualized). This consideration points to something we have to deal with in the last chapter, namely the dependence of the whole realm of moral action on the presence of the Spiritual power.

The relation of justice to love in personal encounters can adequately be described through three functions of creative justice, namely, listening, giving, forgiving. In none of them does love do more than justice demands, but in each of them love recognizes what justice demands. In order to know what is just in a person-to-person encounter, love listens. It is its first task to listen. No human relation, especially no intimate one, is possible without mutual listening. Reproaches, reactions, defences may be justified in terms of proportional justice. But perhaps they would prove to be unjust if there were more mutual listening. All things and all men, so to speak, call on us with small or loud voices. They want us to listen, they want us to understand their intrinsic claims, their justice of being. They want justice from us. But we can give it to them only through the love which listens.

Love in its attempt to see what is in the other person is by no means irrational. It uses all possible means to penetrate into the dark places of his motives and inhibitions. It uses, for example, the tools provided by depth psychology which give unexpected possibilities of discovering the intrinsic claims of a human being. Through it we have learned that human expressions can mean something quite different from what they seem or are intended to mean. They seem to be aggressive, but what they express may be love, inhibited by shyness. They seem to be sweet and submissive and they are actually symptoms of hostility. Words, well meant, but uttered improperly, may produce in reaction complete injustice. Listening love is the first step to justice in person-to-person encounters. And it has also a function in encounters with living nature and nature generally. But if we tried to pursue the problem of human justice and injustice towards nature, a large new field of inquiry would be opened, too large for our present task and too much in need of references to art and poetry for an ontological analysis.

The second function of creative justice in personal encounters is giving. It belongs to the right of everyone whom we encounter to demand something from us, at least that even in the most impersonal relations the other one is acknowledged as a person. But this minimum of giving drives toward a maximum—including possible self-sacrifice if the occasion demands it. Giving is an expression of creative justice if it serves the purpose of reuniting love. It is obvious that under this criterion it may mean the demand to resist and to restrain and to deprive. Here again psychological wisdom can help to do what appears to be the opposite of giving love. Creative justice includes the possibility of sacrificing the other one in his existençe, though not in his being as a person.

The third and most paradoxical form in which justice is united with love is forgiving. Their unity is indicated in the Pauline term: justification by grace. Justification literally means: making just, and it means in the context of Paul's and Luther's doctrine to accept as just him who is unjust. Nothing seems to contradict more the idea of justice than this doctrine, and everybody who has pronounced it has been accused of promoting injustice and amorality. It seems to be utterly unjust to declare him who is unjust, just. But nothing less than this is what has been called the good news in Christian preaching. And nothing less than this is the fulfilment of justice. For it is the only way of reuniting those who are estranged by guilt. Without reconciliation there is no reunion. Forgiving love is the only way of fulfilling the intrinsic claim in every being, namely its claim to be reaccepted into the unity to which it belongs. Creative justice demands that this claim be accepted and that he be accepted who is unacceptable in terms of proportional justice. In accepting him into the unity of forgiveness, love exposes both the acknowledged break with justice on his side with all its implicit consequences and the claim inherent in him to be *declared* just and to be *made* just by reunion.

The unity of justice and power in personal encounters

In any encounter of man with man, power is active, the power of the personal radiation, expressed in language and gestures, in the glance of the eye and the sound of the voice, in face and figure and movement, expressed in what one is personally and what one represents socially. Every encounter, whether friendly or hostile, whether benevolent or indifferent, is in some way, unconsciously or consciously, a struggle of power with power. In this struggle decisions are made continuously about the relative power of being, actualized in all those who are involved in the struggle. Creative justice does not deny these encounters and the conflicts implicit in them. For this is the price which must be paid for the creativity of life. Such struggles start in the life of an individual in the moment of his conception and go on up to the moment of his last breath. They permeate his relations to everything and everybody he encounters. Justice is the form in which these struggles lead to ever-changing decisions about the power of being in each of the struggling beings. The impression given by this picture, the truth of which can hardly be denied, is the complete dependence of justice in personal encounters on the power relation between person and person. But this impression is false because it does not take into consideration that every being which enters the struggle of power with power has already a definite power of being. It is a plant and not a stone, a beast and not a tree, a man and not a dog, a female and not a male. These and innumerable other qualities are given before the struggle in the personal encounter starts and they are the basis for the intrinsic claim for justice, which every being has. But this claim has a large margin of indefiniteness, rooted in the dynamic side of every power of being. And it is this undefined element in the power of a being about which new decisions are always made

This of course is also the source of all injustice. If the new decisions destroy the essential claim of a being, they are unjust. It is not unjust that in the struggle between power and power one of the beings involved shows a superior power of being. The manifestation of this fact is not unjust but creative. But injustice occurs if in this struggle the superior power uses its power for the reduction or destruction of the inferior power. This can happen in all forms of personal encounters. Most frequent are those forms in which the personal encounter occurs within the frame of an institutional structure and the preservation and growth of the institution gives the pretext for unjust compulsion.

There is unjust psychological compulsion in family relations, in educational relations and in all other authority relations. It often happens that parents who look at a young child with an especially severe or angry expression become responsible for a life-long abnormal anxiety of the child. It feels rejected and loses any self-assurance concerning the power and justice of its own being. Its just claims are repressed or transformed into unjust ones, e.g. unconscious destructiveness against itself or against others. This, on the other hand, gives the parents a feeling of being resisted or avoided by the child. Their intrinsic claim as parents is not fulfilled either. Authority can, besides its external compulsory power, exercise a psychological compulsion which conflicts with the justice of person-to-person encounters. Here the large problem arises as to whether there is a type of authority which is, by its very nature, unjust, and another one which is by its very nature just. This seems to be the case: there is 'authority in principle' and there is 'authority in fact'. Authority in principle means that a person has authority by the place he occupies and that he is beyond criticism because of this place. So—to give the most famous example—the Pope as Pope is ultimate authority for every Catholic believer. Thus, the Bible as Bible is ultimate authority for every orthodox Protestant. Thus, the dictator as dictator is ultimate authority in a totalitarian system. Thus, parents are authority for infants and try to remain in this place for ever. So teachers become authorities for pupils without trying to liberate the pupils from their authority. All this 'authority in principle' is unjust authority. It disregards the intrinsic claim of human beings to become responsible for ultimate decisions. Quite different is the 'authority in fact' which is exercised as well as accepted by each of us in every moment. It is an expression of the mutual dependence of all of us on each other; it is an expression of the finite and fragmentary character of our being, of the limits of our power to stand by ourselves. For this reason it is a just authority.

This situation is mirrored in our educational system. One must ask whether education for adjustment is not injustice because it prevents the intrinsic claim for independence from ever coming to the surface. One must ask whether adjustment is not a method of overpowering and therefore essentially injustice. The answer must be that education for adjustment is just in so far as it is a way of giving a form to the individual. It is unjust in so far as it inhibits the individual from creating new forms.

At the end of this chapter I want to point to the fact that a large part of the Existentialist revolt in the creative culture of the last one hundred years is an attempt to provide justice for the individual and to support his intrinsic claim to transcend adjustment by creativity.

VI

THE UNITY OF POWER, JUSTICE, AND LOVE IN GROUP RELATIONS

THE fifth chapter dealt with justice, love, and power in human relations. It was always the relation of man to man which we analysed in its different forms and problems. But no human relation exists in an empty space. There is always a social structure behind it. Therefore we must first speak about:

Structures of power in nature and society

In the analysis of power, it was the power of the individual being in his relation to other individual beings which we tried to understand. This was not possible without references to embracing wholes which give or refuse justice to the individual and which establish rules of just behaviour, such as traditions, customs, and laws. But it was not the life of the groups as such in which we were interested. Now we must turn our attention to this most actual realm.

Structures of power are always centred in inorganic beings like crystals, molecules, atoms, as well as in organic beings. In the latter ones the centredness increases and reaches in man the state of self-consciousness. Then a new centred structure appears; the social group, or, as it is called if it has a manifest centre, a social organism. An organism is the more developed and has a greater power of being, the more different elements are united around an acting centre. Therefore, man produces the richest, most universal and most powerful social organisms. But the individuals who constitute this organism are each independent centres for themselves, and so they can resist the unity of the social organism to which they belong. And here the limits of the analogy between biological and social organisms becomes visible. In a biological organism the parts are nothing without the whole to which they belong. This is not the case in social organisms. The destiny of an individual who is separated from the group to which he belongs may be miserable but the separation is not necessarily fatal. The fate of a limb which is cut off from the living organism to which it belongs is decay. In this sense no human group is an organism in the biological sense. Neither is the family the cell of a quasi-biological organism, nor is the nation something like a biological organism.

This statement is politically significant. Those who like to speak of social organisms do it usually with a reactionary tendency. They want to keep dissenting groups in conformity and they use for this purpose biological metaphors in a literal sense. Prussian conservatism and Roman Catholic family glorification agree at this point. But the individual person is not a limb of a body; he is an ultimate, independent reality, with both personal and social functions. The individual man is a social being, but the society does not create the individual. They are interdependent.

This decides also against the widespread method of personifying a group. A State has often been described as a person who has emotions, thoughts, intentions, decisions like an individual person. But there is a difference which makes all this impossible: the social organism does not have an organic centre, in which the whole being is united so that central deliberations and decisions are possible. The centre of a social group is those who represent it, the rulers or the parliaments, or those who have the real power behind the scene without being official representatives. The analogy has been driven to the point where the representative centres of social power are equated with the deliberating and deciding centre of a personality. But this is what one could call 'a deception of the metaphor'. The analogy can be carried through metaphorically but not properly. For the deciding centre of a group is always a part of the group. It is not the group which decides, but those who have the power to speak for the group and force their decisions upon all the members of the group. And they may do this without the (at least) silent consent of the group. The importance of this analysis is visible whenever one makes a group responsible for what the deciding centre has forced upon the group. This gives a solution to the painful question of the moral guilt of a nation (e.g. Nazi Germany). It is never the nation which is directly guilty for what is done by the nation. It is always the ruling group. But all individuals in a nation are responsible for the existence of the ruling group. Not many individuals in Germany are directly guilty of Nazi atrocities. But all of them are responsible for the acceptance of a government which was willing and able to do such things. Those who represent the power of a social group are a representative but not an actual centre. A group is not a person.

Nevertheless it has a structure of power. It is centred. Therefore social power is hierarchical power, power in degrees. Social power, centred and therefore hierarchical, has many forms in which it can appear. It can appear in the control of a society by a feudal group, a military caste, a high bureaucracy, an economic upper class, a priestly hierarchy, an individual ruler with or without constitutional restrictions, the ruling committees of a parliament, a revolutionary vanguard.

The ruling group shares the tensions of power, especially the tension between power by acknowledgement and power by enforcement. Both are always present, and no power structure can stand if one of them is lacking. The silent acknowledgement of the people appears when they reflect: 'Those who represent us represent us by divine order or by historical destiny.

No question can be raised about it. No criticism is allowed.' Or: 'Those who represent us are chosen by us: now we must accept them as long as they are in legal power, even if they misuse it, otherwise the system as such with the chances it gives to us also would fall down.' The ruling group is safe as long as this kind of acknowledgement is subconscious or half-conscious—metaphorically speaking, silent. Danger for the system appears if the acknowledgement becomes conscious and doubt must be suppressed. Then the moment may come when the suppression no longer works and a revolutionary situation develops. It is noticeable that even in such a situation the law is valid that power has centred or hierarchical character: the bearers of the revolutionary situation are a small group of people who have decided to withdraw acknowledgement. Marx has called them, with a militaristic image, the vanguard. They are the centre of power in a revolutionary situation, the objects of severest suppression in the pre-revolutionary stage, the ruling group in the post-revolutionary stage.

For enforcement is the other side of the hierarchical power structure. It also works well as long as it works silently in the overwhelming majority of the group. This is done by internalized law, a smooth administration and a conformistic attitude. But this is an ideal case and depends on many favourable factors (e.g. in England). Usually the compulsory element is much stronger. There is an easy deception in the mind of idealists about the situation. They experience the small number of enforcing officials in a big city and that even this small number has to do actual enforcement only occasionally. So they feel the absence of enforcement more than its presence. But most enforcement is done by the threat of enforcement, if it is a real threat. Examples for this can be increased indefinitely even with respect to the best educated citizen (taxes). You cannot remove silent acknowledgement and you cannot remove manifest enforcement from any structure of power.

The ruling minority in a social group are both objects of the silent acknowledgement by the majority and the agents of the enforcement of the law against the wilfulness of any member of the group. This latter position produces all the problems which disturb and possibly ruin a social organism. The situation would be simple, if the law the ruling group is supposed to represent and to enforce were unambiguous. But actually it is burdened with all the ambiguities of justice. An archaic acknowledgement of this fact is the idea that the ruler is above the law, because it is his function to make decisions where the law necessarily remains indefinite. Although modern constitutions avoid an open expression of such a translegal position, they cannot exclude actions of the ruling group which follow the same principle. And this position 'above the law' is neither in ancient nor in modern times a denial of the law. On the contrary, it is meant as a way of making the application of the law possible. The law must be given in a creative act, and it is given by members of the ruling group. It must be applied to the concrete situation in a daring decision, and the decision is made by members of the ruling group. It must be changed in a foreseeing risk; and the risk is taken by members of the ruling group. This analysis shows that those who are in power always do two things: they express the power and justice of being of the whole group; and, at the same time, they express the power and the claim for justice of themselves as the ruling group. This situation has induced Christian as well as Marxist anarchists to accept the ideal of a society without a power structure. But being without a power structure means being without a centre of action. It means an agglomeration of individuals without a united power of being and without a uniting form of justice. A State-like organization cannot be avoided, and if it is given, no checks and balances, not even those of the American Constitution, can prevent the ruling groups from expressing their own power and justice of being in the justice and power of the whole group. Those who belong to the ruling group pay a price for it and have a justification for it. They pay the price of identifying their own destiny with the destiny of the whole group. The power of being of the group constitutes their own power of being. They stand and fall with it. And they have the justification that they are acknowledged by the whole group in whatever constitutional terms this may be expressed. They cannot exist if the whole group definitely withdraws its acknowledgement. They can prolong their power by physical and psychological compulsion, but not for ever.

The silent acknowledgement received by a ruling group from the whole group cannot be understood without an element which is derived neither from justice nor from power but from love, namely from love under guidance of its *erōs* and *philia* qualities. It is the experience of community within the group. Every social group is a community, potentially and actually; and the ruling minority not only expresses the power and justice of being of the group, it also expresses the communal spirit of the group, its ideals and valuations. Every organism, natural as well as social, is a power of being and a bearer of an intrinsic claim for justice because it is based on some form of reuniting love. It removes as organism the separatedness of some parts of the world. The cell of a living body, the members of a family, the citizens of a nation, are examples. This communal self-affirmation, on the human level, is called the spirit of the group. The spirit of the group is expressed in all its utterances, in its laws and institutions, in its symbols and myths, in its ethical and cultural forms. It is normally represented by the ruling classes. And this very fact is perhaps the most solid foundation of their power. Every member of the group sees in the members of the ruling minority the incarnation of those ideals which he affirms when he affirms the group to which he belongs. This incarnation may be a king or a bishop, a big landowner or a big business man, a union leader or a revolutionary hero. Therefore every ruling minority preserves and presents and propagates those symbols in which the spirit of the group is expressed. They guarantee the permanence of a power structure more than the strictest methods of enforcement. They guarantee what I have called the silent acknowledgement of the ruling group by the whole group. In this way, the power and justice of being in a social group is dependent on the spirit of the community, and this means on the uniting love which creates and sustains the community.

Power, justice, and love in the encounter of social groups

In our description of the encounter of power of being with power of being we have limited our task to the encounter of individuals with individuals. We must now extend our description to the encounter of social groups with social groups. If we do so we find the same marks of power encounters, the pushing ahead and withdrawing, the absorbing and throwing out, the amalgamation and separation. This is unavoidable.

For every power group experiences growth and disintegration. It tries to transcend itself and to preserve itself at the same time. Nothing is determined *a priori*. It is a matter of trial, risk, and decision. And this trial has elements of intrinsic power united with compulsion whether the group or their representatives want it or not. These encounters are the basic material of history. In them man's political destiny is decided. What is their character? The basis of all power of a social group is the space it must provide for itself. Being means having space or, more exactly, providing space for oneself. This is the reason for the tremendous importance of geographical space and the fight for its possession by all power groups. Our time gives a striking example for this fact. In the necessity of having space the Zionist fight is rooted. Israel lost its independent power of being and often its power of being altogether, when it lost its space. Now it has its space and has shown a rather strong power of being. But perhaps something is lost: the intimate relation to time which made Israel the elected nation and which belongs to the problem of the resignation of power.

The struggle about space is not simply the attempt to remove another group from a given space. The real purpose is to draw this space into a larger power field, to deprive it of a centre of its own. If this happens, it is not the individual power of being which has changed, but the way in which the individual participates in the centre, in which way he influences the law and the spiritual substance of the new, larger power organization.

It is, however, not only geographical space which gives power and being to a social organism. It is also the radiation of power into the larger space of mankind. One of these radiations which enlarge one's own space without reducing that of others is economic expansion. Another one is technical expansion or the spread of science and civilization. In none of these cases is a preceding calculation possible. Every factor is changing, the number of the population, the productive power, new discoveries, movements, emigration, competition, the rise of new countries, the disintegration of old ones. History, so to speak, tries what will be its next constellation. And in these trials nations and empires are sacrificed, and others are called into existence. The power of being of each political power group is measured by its encounter with the power of being of other power groups.

But now we must remember that power is never only physical force, but it is also the power of symbols and ideas in which the life of a social group expresses itself. The consciousness of such a spiritual substance *can* become, and in the most important cases of history *does* become, the feeling of a special vocation. If we look at European history we find a series of expressions of such a vocational consciousness, and we find tremendous historical consequences following from it. In an indistinguishable unity of power drive and vocational consciousness the Romans subjected the Mediterranean world to the Roman law and the order of the Roman empire, based on this law. In the same way Alexander brought Greek culture to nations which were subjected in terms of both arms and language. Considering the fact that these two imperial drives in their amalgamation created the *oikoumenē*, the condition and frame of the spread of Christianity, we cannot say that their vocational consciousness was wrong. The same must be said about the medieval German Empire, which, on the basis of the power drives of the Germanic tribes and the vocational consciousness of the Germanic kings, created the structure for the united Christian body with all the glory of medieval religion and culture. After the end of the Middle Ages the European nations combined power drives with vocational consciousness of different character. Spain's world-conquering imperialism was united with the fanatical belief in being the divine tool of the Counter-Reformation. England's vocational consciousness was rooted partly in the Calvinistic idea of world politics for the preservation of pure Christianity, partly in a Christian-humanistic feeling of responsibility for the colonial countries and for a solid balance of power between the civilized nations. This was inseparably united with an economic and political power drive and produced the largest Empire of all

times and almost eighty years of European peace. The
vocational consciousness of France was based on its
cultural superiority in the seventeenth and eighteenth
centuries. Modern Germany was under the impact
of the so-called *Real-Politik*, without a vocational
consciousness. Her ideology was the struggle for
Lebensraum, partly in competition with the colonial
nations and therefore in conflict with them. Hitler's
use of an obviously absurd vocational idea, that of
Nordic blood, was artificially imposed and only
reluctantly accepted, because there was no genuine
vocational symbol. To-day two great imperialistic
systems fight with each other in terms of both force and
vocational consciousness: Russia and America. The
Russian vocational consciousness was based on its
religious feeling that it had a mission towards the
West, namely, to save the disintegrating Western
civilization through Eastern mystical Christianity.
This was the claim of the Slavophile movement in the
nineteenth century. Present-day Russia has a similar
missionary consciousness towards the West and at the
same time towards the Far East. Her power drive,
which in the official counter-propaganda appears as
the desire for world domination, is not understandable
without her fanatical vocational consciousness, which
must be compared with that of all other imperialistic
movements. America's vocational consciousness has
been called 'the American dream', namely to establish

the earthly form of the kingdom of God by a new beginning. The old forms of oppressive power were left
behind and a new start was made. In the Constitution
and the living democracy (both are quasi-religious
concepts in the United States) the will is embodied
to actualize what is felt as the American vocation.
This was originally meant for America alone. Now
it is meant explicitly for one-half of the world and
implicitly for the whole world. The actual power
drive working together with this vocational feeling
is still rather limited. But the historical situation increases it more and more. And it is already justified to
speak of half-conscious American imperialism.

Vocational consciousness expresses itself in laws. In
these laws both justice and love are actual. The justice
of the empires is not only ideology or rationalization.
The empires not only subject, they also unite. And
in so far as they are able to do this, they are not without
love. Therefore those who are subjected acknowledge
silently that they have become participants of a superior
power of being and meaning. If this acknowledgement
vanishes because the uniting power of the empire, its
strength, and its vocational idea vanish, the empire
comes to an end. Its power of being disintegrates and
external attacks only execute what is already decided.

The present decrease in national sovereignty, the
rise of embracing power groups, and the split of the
world into two all-embracing systems of political

power raises naturally the problem of a united mankind. What can be derived from our analysis of power, justice, and love for this question?

There are three answers to this question. The first one does not recognize the inescapable character of the recent developments towards larger organisms of power and expects a return to a number of relatively independent power centres, perhaps not national but continental. The second answer seeks for the solution in a world state, created by a kind of federal union of the present main powers and by their subjection to a central authority in which all groups participate. The third answer expects that one of the great powers will develop into a world centre, ruling the other nations through liberal methods and in democratic forms! The first answer is a matter of foresight. It belongs to the movement of social organisms that the centralizing tendency is always balanced by a decentralizing one. The question is: Which tendency determines the present situation? The technical union of the world favours centralization, but there are other, above all psychological, factors which may prevail. The second answer, the expectation of the world state, contradicts the analysis of power as we have given it. A power centre which unites strength with vocational consciousness cannot subject itself to an artificial authority without both of them. The presupposition for a political world unity is the presence of a spiritual unity expressed in symbols and myths. Nothing like this exists to-day. And before it does exist a world state has no power to create silent acknowledgement. The most probable answer seems to be the third one. It may well be that after the period of world history which is characterized by the rise of *one* power structure to universal power, with a minimum of suppression, the law and the justice and the uniting love which are embodied in this power will become the universal power of mankind. But even then the kingdom of God has not come upon us. For even then disintegration and revolution are not excluded. New centres of power may appear, first underground, then openly, driving towards separation from or towards radical transformation of the whole. They may develop a vocational consciousness of their own.

Then the power struggle starts again and the period of the fulfilled world empire will be as limited as the Augustan period of peace was. Can uniting love never unite mankind? Can mankind never become as a whole a structure of power and a source of universal justice? With this question we have left the realm of history and approach the question of love, power, and justice in their relation to that which is ultimate.

VII

THE UNITY OF LOVE, POWER, AND JUSTICE IN THE ULTIMATE RELATION

THE first four chapters have developed the main thesis of this book directly. They have tried to show that without ontological foundation neither love nor power nor justice can be adequately interpreted. The two following chapters have confirmed this thesis indirectly by applying the results of the ontological analysis to the problem of justice in personal relations and to the problem of power in group relations. If in this way the ontological character of love, power, and justice is established the question of their theological character immediately arises. For the ontological and the theological are in one point identical: both deal with being as being. The first assertion to be made about God is that He is being-itself.

The theological question has already entered our discussion at several points. It has been anticipated by the description of life as separation and reunion, or as love. Such a description of life is strictly analogous to the trinitarian interpretation of the living God. In his Son, God separates Himself from Himself, and in the Spirit He reunites Himself with Himself. This, of course, is a symbolic way of speaking, but it reminds

Christians always of the truth that God is not dead identity but the living ground of everything that has life. Beyond this, we referred to the *agapē* quality of love as that which is emphasized in the New Testament. We spoke of the divine justice, both in its natural aspect, according to which everything has its intrinsic claim for justice, and in the aspect of forgiving and reuniting justice. We referred to man's resistance against reuniting love, his estrangement from himself, from other beings, and from the ground of his being. And we protested against a doctrine of God in which God is made powerless; for being must be described as the power of being.

All this shows that no discussion of concepts like love, power, and justice, is possible without touching the dimension of ultimate concern, the dimension of the holy.

But there is a profounder reason for the necessity of reaching into this dimension. It was our task to show that essentially, in their created nature, love, power, and justice are united. This, however, was not possible without showing that in existence they are separated and conflicting. This leads to the question: How can their essential unity be re-established? The answer is obvious: Through the manifestation of the ground in which they are united. Love, power, and justice are one in the divine ground, they shall become one in human existence. The holy in which they are united shall become holy reality in time and space. How and in which sense is this possible?

God as the source of love, power, and justice

The basic assertion about the relation of God to love, power, and justice is made, if one says that God is being itself. For being itself, according to our ontological analysis, implies love as well as power and justice. God is the basic and universal symbol for what concerns us ultimately. As being-itself He is ultimate reality, the really real, the ground and abyss of everything that is real. As the God, with whom I have a person-to-person encounter, He is the subject of all the symbolic statements in which I express my ultimate concern. Everything we say about being-itself, the ground and abyss of being, must be symbolic. It is taken out of the material of our finite reality and applied to that which transcends the finite infinitely. Therefore it cannot be used in its literal sense. To say anything about God in the literal sense of the words used means to say something false about Him. The symbolic in relation to God is not less true than the literal, but it is the only true way of speaking about God.

This refers also to the three ideas we are discussing. If we speak of God as loving or, more emphatically, of God as being love, we use our experience of love and our analysis of life as the material which alone we can use. But we also know that if we apply it to God we throw it into the mystery of the divine depth, where it is transformed without being lost. It is still love, but it is now divine love. This does not mean that a higher being has in a fuller sense what we call love, but it does mean that our love is rooted in the divine life, i.e. in something which transcends our life infinitely in being and meaning.

The same we must say of the divine power. It is applied to God symbolically. We experience power in physical acts as well as in the ability to carry through our will against contradicting wills. This experience is the material we use when we speak of the divine power. We speak of His omnipotence and we address Him as the Almighty. Literally taken, this would mean that God is a highest being, who can do what He wants to do, the implication being that there are a lot of things which He does not want to do, a concept which leads into a fog of absurd imaginations. The real meaning of almightiness is that God is the power of being in everything that is, transcending every special power infinitely but acting at the same time as its creative ground. In the religious experience the power of God provokes the feeling of being in the hand of a power which cannot be conquered by any other power, in ontological terms, which is the infinite resistance against non-being and the eternal victory over it. To participate in this resistance and this victory is felt as the way to overcome the threat of non-being which is the destiny of everything finite. In every prayer to the almighty God, power is seen in the light of the divine power. It is seen as ultimate reality.

Justice is applied to God equally in an ultimate and therefore symbolic sense. God is symbolized as the righteous judge who judges according to the law He has given. This is the material taken out of our experience. It also must be thrown into the mystery of the divine life and in it both preserved and transformed. It has become a true symbol of the relation of the ground of being to that which is grounded in it, especially to man. The divine law is beyond the alternative of natural and positive law. It is the structure of reality and of everything in it, including the structure of the human mind. In so far as it is this, it is natural law, the law of continuous creation, the justice of being in everything. At the same time it is positive law, posited by God in His freedom which is not dependent on any given structure outside Him. In so far as it is natural law, we can understand the law in nature and mankind and formulate it deductively. In so far as it is positive law we have to accept what is given to us empirically and we have to observe it inductively. Both sides are rooted in God's relation to the justice in things.

To see love, power, and justice as true symbols of the divine life, means to see their ultimate unity. Unity is not identity. An element of separation is presupposed when we speak of unity. There are present, in the symbolic application of our three concepts to God, also some symbols of tension.

The first is the tension between love and power. The exclamation has been and will be repeated innumerably: How can an all-powerful God who is, at the same time the God of love, allow such misery? Either He has not sufficient love or He has not sufficient power. As an emotional outburst this question is very understandable. As a theoretical formulation it is rather poor. If God had produced a world in which physical and moral evil were impossible, the creatures would not have had the independence of God which is presupposed in the experience of reuniting love. The world would have become a paradise of dreaming innocence, an infant's paradise, but neither love, nor power nor justice would have become real. Actualization of one's potentialities includes, unavoidably, estrangement; estrangement from one's essential being, so that we may find it again in maturity. Only a God who is like a foolish mother, who is so afraid about the well-being of her child that she keeps him in a state of enforced innocence and enforced participation in her own life, could have kept the creatures in the prison of a dreaming paradise. And, as in the case of the mother, this would have been hidden hostility and not love. And it would not have been power either. The power of God is that He overcomes estrangement, not that

He prevents it; that He takes it, symbolically speaking, upon Himself, not that He remains in a dead identity with Himself. This is the meaning of the age-old symbol of the god participating in creaturely suffering, a symbol which in Christianity was applied to the interpretation of the Cross of Him who was said to be the Christ. This is the unity of love and power in the depth of reality itself, power not only in its creative element but also in its compulsory element and the destruction and suffering connected with it. These considerations give theology a key to the eternal problem of theodicy, the problem of the relation of the divine love and the divine power to non-being, namely to death, guilt, and meaninglessness. The ontological unity of love and power is this key which certainly does not open up the mystery of being but which can replace some rusty keys to misleading doors.

While the tension between love and power refers basically to creation, the tension between love and justice refers basically to salvation. The analysis of transforming justice as an expression of creative love makes it unnecessary for me to reject the ordinary contrast between proportional justice and super-added love. In this sense, there can be no conflict between justice and love in God. But in another sense there could be, in a sense which is very similar to that in which love and power have been contrasted. Love destroys, as its strange work, what is against love. It does so according to the justice without which it would be chaotic surrender of the power of being. Love, at the same time, as its own work, saves through forgiveness that which is against love. It does so according to the justifying paradox without which it would be a legal mechanism. How can these two works of love be one? They are one because love does not enforce salvation. If it did it would commit a double injustice. It would disregard the claim of every person to be treated not as a thing but as a centred, deciding, free, and responsible self. Since God is love and His love is one with His power, He has not the power to force somebody into His salvation. He would contradict Himself. And this God cannot do. At the same time such an act would disregard the strange work of love, namely the destruction of what destroys love. It would violate the unconditioned character of love and with it the divine majesty. Love must destroy what is against love, but not him who is the bearer of that which is against love. For as a creature, he remains a power of being or a creation of love. But the unity of his will is destroyed, he is thrown into a conflict with himself, the name of which is despair, mythologically speaking, hell. Dante was right when he called even Hell a creation of the divine love. The hell of despair is the strange work that love does within us in order to open us up for its own work, justification of him who is unjust. But even despair does not make us into a mechanism. It is a test of our freedom and personal dignity, even in relation to God. The Cross of Christ is the symbol of the divine love, participating in the destruction into which it throws him who acts against love: This is the meaning of atonement.

Love, power, and justice are one in God. But we must ask: What do love, power, and justice do within an estranged world?

Love, power, and justice in the holy community

Love, power, and justice are united in God and they are united in the new creation of God in the world. Man is estranged from the ground of his being, from himself and from his world. But he is still man. He cannot completely cut the tie with his creative ground, he is still a centred person and in this sense united with himself. He still participates in his world. In other words: The reuniting love, the power of resisting non-being, and the creative justice are still active in him. Life is not unambiguously good. Then it would not be life but only the possibility of life. And life is not unambiguously evil. Then non-being would have conquered being. But life is ambiguous in all its expressions. It is ambiguous also with respect to love, power, and justice. We have touched on this fact in many places in our previous discussions. We must now consider it in the light of the new creation within the world of estrangement, which I suggest calling the holy community.

In an anticipating summary I would say: in the holy community the *agapē* quality of love cuts into the *libido*, *erōs*, and *philia* qualities of love and elevates them beyond the ambiguities of their self-centredness. In the holy community the spiritual power, by surrendering compulsion, elevates power beyond the ambiguities of its dynamic realization. In the holy community justification by grace elevates justice beyond the ambiguities of its abstract and calculating nature. This means that in the holy community love, power, and justice in their ontological structure are affirmed but that their estranged and ambiguous reality is transformed into a manifestation of their unity within the divine life.

Let us first consider the ambiguities of love and the work of love as *agapē* in the holy community. Libido is good in itself! We have defended it against Freud's depreciation of what he described as the infinite libidinous drive with its ensuing dissatisfaction and death instinct. We have accepted this as the description in estrangement, but not of libido in its creative meaning. Without libido life would not move beyond itself. The Bible knows this as well as recent depth psychology, and we should be grateful that our new insights into the deeper levels of human nature have rediscovered the Biblical realism which was covered by several strata of idealistic and moralistic self-deception about man. Biblical realism knows both that libido belongs to man's created goodness and that it is distorted and ambiguous in the state of man's estrangement. Libido has become unlimited and has fallen under the tyranny of the pleasure principle. It uses the other being not as an object of reunion but as a tool for gaining pleasure out of him. Sexual desire is not evil as desire, and the breaking of conventional laws is not evil as the breaking of conventional laws, but sexual desire and sexual autonomy are evil if they bypass the centre of the other person—in other words, if they are not united with the two other qualities of love, and if they are not under the ultimate criterion of the *agapē* quality of love. *Agapē* seeks the other one in his centre. *Agapē* sees him as God sees him. *Agapē* elevates libido into the divine unity of love, power, and justice.

The same is true of *erōs*. We have, following Plato, defined *erōs* as the driving force in all cultural creativity and in all mysticism. As such *erōs* has the greatness of a divine-human power. It participates in creation and in the natural goodness of everything created. But it also participates in the ambiguities of life. The *erōs* quality of love can be confused with the libido quality and be drawn into its ambiguities. Witness for this is the fact that the New Testament could not use the word *erōs* any more because of its predominantly sexual connotations. And even the mystical *erōs* can express itself in symbols which are not only taken from the sexual life but which draw the love to God to an openly ascetic, hiddenly sexual level. But more is involved when we speak of the ambiguity of the *erōs* quality of love. It is the aesthetic detachment which can take hold of our relation to culture and makes *erōs* ambiguous. We have learned this especially from Kierkegaard. His aesthetic stage of man's spiritual development is not a stage but a universal quality of love exposed to the dangers Kierkegaard describes. The ambiguity of cultural *erōs* is its detachment from the realities which it expresses and consequently the disappearing of existential participation and ultimate responsibility. The wings of *erōs* become wings of escape. Culture is irresponsibly enjoyed. It has not received the justice which it can demand. *Agapē* cuts into the detached safety of a merely aesthetic *erōs*. It does not deny the longing toward the good and the true and its divine source, but it prevents it from becoming an aesthetic enjoyment without ultimate seriousness. *Agapē* makes the cultural *erōs* responsible and the mystical *erōs* personal.

The ambiguities of the *philia* quality of love appeared already in its first description as person-to-person love between equals. However large the group of equals may be, the *philia* quality of love establishes preferential love. Some are preferred, the majority are excluded. This is obvious not only in intimate relations as family and friendship, but also in the innumerable forms of sympathetic person-to-person encounters. The implicit or explicit rejection of all those who are not admitted to such a preferential relation is negative compulsion and can be as cruel as any compulsion. But such a rejection of others is tragically unavoidable. Nobody can escape the necessity to exercise it. There are special forms of love with *philia* quality which the psychoanalyst Erich Fromm has called symbiotic relation and which make this tragic necessity rather clear. If the one partner of a *philia*-relation is used by the other one either for the sake of masochistic dependence or of sadistic domination or of both in interdependence, something which seemed to be friendship of highest quality is in reality compulsion without justice. Again, *agapē* does not deny the preferential love of the *philia* quality, but it purifies it from a subpersonal bondage, and it elevates the preferential love into universal love. The preferences of friendship are not negated, but they do not exclude, in a kind of aristocratic self-separation, all the others. Not everybody is a friend, but everybody is affirmed as a person. *Agapē* cuts through the separation of equals and unequals, of sympathy and antipathy, of friendship and indifference, of desire and disgust. It needs no sympathy in order to love; it loves what it has to reject in terms of *philia*. *Agapē* loves in everybody and through everybody love itself.

What *agapē* does to the ambiguities of love, Spiritual power does to the ambiguities of natural power. The ambiguities of power are rooted in the dynamic character and the compulsory implications of power. Spiritual power is not the conquest of these ambiguities by resignation of power, because this would mean resignation of being. It would be the attempt to annihilate oneself in order to escape guilt. Spiritual power is not the denial of power dynamics. In many stories about the working of the Spiritual power bodily effects are mentioned, like elevation, removal from one place to the other, shock, and horror. There are always psychological effects visible. Spirit is power, grasping and moving out of the dimension of the ultimate. It is not identical with the realm of ideas or meanings. It is dynamic power, overcoming resistance. Then what is its difference from the other forms of power? The Spiritual power works neither through bodily nor through psychological compulsion. It works through man's total personality, and this means, through him as finite freedom. It does not remove his freedom, but it makes his freedom free from the compulsory elements which limit it. The Spiritual power gives a centre to the whole personality, a centre which transcends the whole personality and, consequently, is independent of any of its elements. And this is ultimately the only way of uniting the personality with itself. If this happens man's natural or social power of being becomes irrelevant. He may keep them, he may resign some of them or even of all of them. The Spiritual power works through them or it works through the surrender of them. He may exercise Spiritual power through words or thought, through what he is and what he does, or through the surrender of them or through the sacrifice of himself. In all these forms he can change reality by attaining levels of being which are ordinarily hidden. This is the power which elevates the holy community above the ambiguities of power.

I do not need to say much about the relation of grace and justice. The act of forgiving has been mentioned in connexion with the encounter of person and person. Mutual forgiveness is the fulfilment of creative justice. But mutual forgiveness is justice only if it is based on reuniting love, in justification by grace. Only God can forgive, because in Him alone love and justice are completely united. The ethics of forgiveness are rooted in the message of divine forgiveness. Otherwise they are delivered to the ambiguities of justice, oscillating between legalism and sentimentality. In the holy community this ambiguity is conquered.

Agapē conquers the ambiguities of love, Spiritual power conquers the ambiguities of power, grace conquers the ambiguities of justice. This is true not only of the encounters of man with man, but also in the encounter of man with himself. Man can love himself in terms of self-acceptance only if he is certain that he is accepted. Otherwise his self-acceptance is self-complacency and arbitrariness. Only in the light and in the power of the 'love from above' can he love himself. This implies the answer to the question of man's justice towards himself. He can be just towards himself only in so far as ultimate justice is done to him, namely the condemning, forgiving, and giving judgement of 'justification'. The condemning element in justification makes self-complacency impossible, the forgiving element saves from self-condemnation and despair, the giving element provides for a Spiritual centre which unites the elements of our personal self and makes power over oneself possible.

Justice, power, and love towards oneself is rooted in the justice, power, and love which we receive from that which transcends us and affirms us. The relation to ourselves is a function of our relation to God.

The last question put before us has been asked at the end of the chapter on the relation between social power groups. It was the question of the reunion of mankind in terms of love, power, and justice. No answer could be given on the level of political organization. Is there an answer out of the relation to the ultimate?

It is the merit of pacifism that, in spite of its theological shortcomings, it has kept this question alive in modern Christianity. Without it the Churches probably would have forgotten the torturing seriousness of any religious affirmation of war. On the other hand, pacifism has usually restricted a much larger problem of human existence to the question of war. But there are other questions of equal seriousness in the same sphere. One of them is the question of armed conflicts within a power group, always going on potentially in the use of police and armed forces for the preservation of order, sometimes coming into the open in revolutionary wars. If successful, they are later on called 'glorious revolutions'. Does the union of mankind mean that not only national but also revolutionary wars are excluded? And if so, has the dynamics of life come to an end; and does this mean that life itself has come to an end?

One can ask the same question with respect to the dynamics of the economic life. Even in a static society such as that of the Middle Ages, the economic dynamics were important and had tremendous historical consequences. One should remain aware of the fact that often more destruction and suffering is produced by economic than by military battles. Should the economic dynamics be stopped and a static world system of production and consumption be introduced? If this were so the whole technical process would also have to be stopped, life in most realms would have to be organized in ever-repeated processes. Every disturbance would have to be avoided. Again the dynamics of life and with it life itself would have come to an end.

Let us assume for a moment that this were possible. Under an unchangeable central authority all encounters of power with power are regulated. Nothing is risked, everything decided. Life has ceased to transcend itself. Creativity has come to an end. The history of man would be finished, post-history would have started. Mankind would be a flock of blessed animals without dissatisfaction, without drive into the future. The horrors and sufferings of the historical period would be remembered as the dark ages of mankind. And then it might happen that one or the other of these blessed men would feel a longing for these past ages, their misery and their greatness, and would force a new beginning of history upon the rest.

This image will show that a world without the dynamics of power and the tragedy of life and history is not the Kingdom of God, is not the fulfilment of man and his world. Fulfilment is bound to eternity and no imagination can reach the eternal. But fragmentary anticipations are possible. The Church itself is such a fragmentary anticipation. And there are groups and movements, which although they do not belong to the manifest Church, represent something we may call a 'latent Church'. But neither the manifest nor the latent Church is the Kingdom of God.

Many problems connected with the all-embracing subject of this book have not been mentioned at all. Others have been touched on only briefly, and others have been treated rather inadequately. However, I hope that the preceding chapters have proved one thing: that the problems of love, power, and justice categorically demand an ontological foundation and a theological view in order to be saved from the vague talk, idealism, and cynicism with which they are usually treated. Man cannot solve any of his great problems if he does not see them in the light of his own being and of being-itself.

INDEX